Books by the Authors

BY JON CARLSON

Elementary School Guidance and Counseling (with William H. Van Hoose and John J. Pietrofesa)

Consulting: Facilitating Human Potential and Change Processes (with Don Dinkmeyer)

The Consulting Process (with Howard Splete and Roy Kern)

Consultation: A Book of Readings (with Don Dinkmeyer)

The Centered Athlete (with Gay Hendricks)

Time for a Better Marriage (with Don Dinkmeyer)

The Growing Teacher (with Casey Thorpe)

PREP for Effective Family Living (with Don Dinkmeyer, Gary McKay, Don C. Dinkmeyer, Jr., and James Dinkmeyer)

Counseling the Adolescent (with Judith Lewis)

BY DON DINKMEYER

Encouraging Children to Learn: The Encouragement Process (with Rudolf Dreikurs)

Child Development: The Emerging Self

Guidance and Counseling in the Elementary School: Readings in Theory and Practice

Developmental Counseling and Guidance: A Comprehensive School Approach (with Edson Caldwell)

Group Counseling: Theory and Practice (with James Muro)

Raising a Responsible Child (with Gary McKay)

Consulting: Facilitating Human Potential and Change Processes (with Jon Carlson)

Consultation: A Book of Readings (with Jon Carlson)

The Parent's Handbook, Systematic Training for Effective Parenting (STEP) (with Gary McKay)

Counseling in the Elementary and Middle School (with James Muro and Don Dinkmeyer, Jr.)

The Encouragement Book: Becoming a Positive Person (with Lew Losoncy)

Systematic Training for Effective Teaching Handbook (with Gary McKay and Don Dinkmeyer, Jr.)

The Parent's Guide, Systematic Training for Effective Parenting of Teens (with Gary McKay)

Time for a Better Marriage (with Jon Carlson)

PREP for Effective Family Living (with Gary McKay, Don Dinkmeyer, Jr., James Dinkmeyer, and Jon Carlson)

The Effective Parent (with Gary McKay, Don Dinkmeyer, Jr., James Dinkmeyer, and Joyce McKay)

Systems of Family Therapy: An Adlerian Integration (with Robert Sherman)

Adlerian Counseling & Psychotherapy, second edition (with Don Dinkmeyer, Jr., and Len Sperry)

Experts Advise Parents: A Guide to Raising Loving, Responsible Children (multiple authors—Edited by Eileen Shiff)

New Beginnings, Parent's Manual, Skills for Single Parents and Stepfamily Parents (with Gary McKay and Joyce McKay)

TAKING TIME FOR LOVE

How to Stay Happily Married

Don Dinkmeyer, Ph.D.

AND

Jon Carlson, Ed.D.

Prentice Hall Press

New York London Toronto Sydney Tokyo

Prentice Hall Press
Gulf+Western Building
One Gulf+Western Plaza
New York, New York 10023

Library of Congress Cataloging-in-Publication Data

Dinkmeyer, Don C.
  Taking time for love : how to stay happily married
Don Dinkmeyer and Jon Carlson.–1st ed.
    p. cm.
  Includes index.
ISBN 0-13-435108-8 (pbk.) : $9.95
  1. Marriage. 2. Love. 3. Interpersonal relations.
I. Carlson, Jon. II. Title.
HQ734.D6248 1989
646.7′8—dc19   88-25154
                                                       CIP

Designed by Victoria Hartman

Manufactured in the United States of America

10 9 8 7 6 5 4 3 2 1

First Edition

*For E. Jane Dinkmeyer and Laura Carlson.
Their patience, encouragement, understanding,
and respect have provided us time for a
loving relationship.*

Contents

Preface

Our professional lives have been devoted to improving human relationships. We have studied psychology and education and hold advanced degrees in both disciplines. We have studied the works of Alfred Adler and believe that training and psychoeducation are often preferable to treatment or, at least, should accompany therapy. People have not had proper training in how to live effectively with one another in today's world. Our pattern of relationships has changed dramatically from the autocratic orientation of a pecking order to a democratic, more equal method of relating. This change has produced conflict and dissatisfaction among people, and these relationship problems have been most pronounced in the area of marriage.

The production of *Training in Marriage Enrichment,* a multimedia marriage-enrichment program, enabled us to work with couples all over the United States and to help them improve their marriage skills. We believe that the problem with marriage today is that couples do not have the skills necessary to maintain effective relationships. Today's world is a very busy one. Couples do not feel that they have time to devote to relationships. We have discovered that brief (about one minute) but powerful exercises, if properly used, can produce major changes in relationships. The activities may appear to be deceptively simple; however, couples who are willing to attempt these exercises on a regular basis will find themselves delightfully surprised.

Taking Time for Love was not created by the authors alone. We thank Mary N. Bregman, PJ Dempsey, E. Jane Dinkmeyer, and Candace Ward Howell for their work on this manuscript. We acknowledge David and Vera Mace for their pioneering work in marriage enrichment and their example of what marriage can be, and the late William H. Van Hoose, who provided us with guidance and friendship. We recognize Bernard Shulman, whose work helped us understand the family system. Finally, we acknowledge Rudolf Dreikurs and Alfred Adler, upon whose ideas the foundation for our work rests.

—Don Dinkmeyer, Coral Springs, FL
—Jon Carlson, Lake Geneva, WI

How to Use This Book

The tasks and exercises in *Taking Time for Love* might appear to be deceptively simple and therefore not worth doing. Try the exercises, however, before deciding on their value. These exercises are constructed to make positive changes in the marital relationship and are based on sound psychotherapeutic principles. Just because they are simple and easy to understand, it does not mean that they are ineffective. It is not important for the reader to clearly understand how these processes work; just enjoy the results.

Most readers will choose to read the book from beginning to end and complete the exercises as they appear; others will choose to use the results of the Marriage Assessment Inventory to structure a program for reading the book. Couples who do the latter may focus first on the chapters and exercises that deal with skills they need to strengthen. Others will start working on areas where they have achieved success in order to maintain positive feelings and to build on these strengths.

Most exercises can be done alone and are designed to be completed without a partner's cooperation; however, a few will require cooperation. It is not necessary for couples to work through the program together. Most readers find the exercises are more effective and the program works best when couples work together. To stay happily married, couples must take time for love. Encourage your spouse to cooperate and work with you. If your partner is not ready, it may be a sign of his or her discouragement. Be patient, accepting, and understanding. Listen to your spouse's feelings and be empathetic. If he or she still chooses not to work with you, remember you can change only yourself. Read the ideas and put them into practice for yourself.

To effectively use the strategies in this book, it is important to allow time each day to work on your marital relationship. Set aside a time each day to read an exercise and design a way to implement it. Many couples find early morning to be their time period; others choose the late afternoon or early evening as their ideal time. Experiment with your own schedules and find your time to apply the skills on a daily basis.

Some people may not feel that an exercise is for them or that it would be "phony" to act in a particular fashion. We urge you to do the exercise anyway, even if it seems to not be "you." Most new behaviors, feelings, and thoughts are uncomfortable and are not "you" initially. With time and practice, however, these skills may fit better into your personality than you initially thought. Keep an open attitude: In order for your relationship to improve, you need to be willing to act differently, or, as the old Chinese proverb states, "If you don't change your direction, you will end up where you're headed."

Seek professional help when you and your spouse both refuse to listen to each other and are too discouraged to see any places where you can be positive and make progress. Many couples who want help with the normal problems of marriage are seeking professional help. Using professional marriage and family therapists and psychologists has lost much of the stigma that it once had. Couples can learn to deepen their understanding of marriage and gain additional relationship skills as the therapist helps them maneuver around defense mechanisms and blind spots.

If you and your partner decide to seek a marriage therapist, choose a professional whose primary area of expertise is in marriage therapy, not individual therapy, so that he or she will be well versed in the complexities of relationships. Insist on seeing the therapist as a couple and focus on couple, rather than individual, issues. The person professing expertise in marriage therapy may be a clergyman, a social worker, a psychologist, or a psychiatrist: Get recommendations from friends, clergy, or your family physician. If you are unable to get a referral, contact the American Association of Marriage and Family Therapists (AAMFT), 1717 K Street, N.W., Washington D.C. 20006; tel.: (202) 429–1825. When you decide on a particular therapist, it's important to check out his or her professional credentials. Make sure that the therapist is fully accredited by a professional organization, such as the American Association of Marriage and Family Therapists, the American Psychological Association, the American Association of Pastoral Counselors, or the American Psychiatric Association.

If you are interested in working with a marriage therapist who is specifically trained in the methods of Adlerian therapy, we suggest that you contact the North American Society of Adlerian Psychology, 202 South State St., Suite 1212, Chicago, IL 60604; tel.: (312) 939–0834. To attend *Training in Marriage Enrichment* workshops, contact the Communication & Motivation Training Institute, Box 8268, Coral Springs, FL 33065.

Many people are very discouraged about their marriage. They feel they have tried but believe that their partner will not cooperate, or that nothing works. Our experience indicates that everyone has the potential to change. Relationships do change when each person takes responsibility for his or her behavior and attitudes and becomes involved while developing skills. Making an effort, recognizing your partner's good intentions and efforts, starts the momentum moving positively. Relationships can be loving and skills can be learned. The choice is up to you!

Time to Show Your Love

Shouldn't marriage be getting better?
Can this marriage be saved?
Can I feel and love like I did during my
courtship?
How can I get my partner to fall in love with
me again?
What are my marriage goals and expectations?
What am I doing in this marriage?
Is what I'm doing helping or hurting?
Is there anything else I can do to improve things
between us?

I f you have ever asked yourself any of these questions, you are not alone. These are the questions people most commonly ask themselves about their marriage. Most married people want to stay married. They understand and want the advantages that a happy marriage can bring: a longer and healthier life, love and acceptance and emotional support, more material goods, successful children, and so on. The problem for most married couples today is *how* to stay married while maintaining a level of satisfaction that makes both partners happy.

Marriage begins on a high note with expressions of love and respect between husband and wife. If this behavior does not continue, however, even the best marriage can spiral downward until each of you treat friends, co-workers, and total strangers with much more respect and caring than you do your spouse. Our work with couples in family therapy has led us to believe that this lack of respect and caring occurs because people do not know what it takes to create and maintain a happy union after the goal of "marriage" has been attained.

When a rift is perceived in the marriage, couples will often try to get closer sexually with the hope that it will bring them together. Physical intimacy is easier to achieve than psychological intimacy, but it does not last, and, if used as the only means of closeness, sex cannot and does not bring happiness. In many marriages sex becomes casual, devoid of true caring and concern. Sex can bring a marriage together only if it is coupled with true psychological intimacy. Psychological intimacy involves caring, concern, and honesty for your spouse, which results in an open exchange of thoughts, beliefs, feelings, hopes, and goals. It is based on a risk-taking approach that allows each person to share openly and honestly. When true psychological intimacy is achieved, couples feel they are moving together to achieve mutual goals and understanding, while still encouraging and supporting each partner's independence.

Many marriages get into trouble because each partner reacts to events and situations on an immediate-need basis without considering the long-term effects of these reactions on the marriage. Couples also create rules (often unspoken) that regulate their existence together. Some common examples are "I must get my way," "If I'm treated unfairly I will get even," "I must be in control," and "Things need to be done perfectly." Often these rules, which influence the couple's behavior patterns, cause each partner pain, and, over time, damage the relationship.

All you need to keep your marriage on track and moving forward are some specific and simple guidelines to follow. Holding daily dialogue sessions with your partner, scheduling weekly marriage meetings, and providing regular encouragement to your partner are ways to invest in a maintenance plan to ensure a fully functioning, satisfying relationship. Such guidelines *are* available and need only to be learned and followed. They do not cost anything, but following them will bring about a profound change in your marriage.

Making Positive Relationship Changes

B. F. Skinner tried to change the world by changing behavior, and Sigmund Freud tried to change the world by explaining and changing people's viewpoints. The model for this book follows the work of Alfred Adler, who changed the whole person—behaviors, thoughts, feelings, and relationships with others. As a couple, you will learn to develop positive *actions,* learn to develop positive *feelings,* and learn how to develop positive *thoughts* about your partner: The end result will be a stronger marital *system.* Increasing sexual intimacy and learning maintenance strategies will keep your marriage alive and growing.

The Importance of Communication

Effective communication is the cornerstone in building a loving relationship. A marriage works best when communication is open, honest, and caring.

In this type of relationship you seek to understand your partner. You communicate with warmth, respect, and positive intentions. Effective communication works to be encouraging; it emphasizes the positive in you and your spouse, as well as the positive potential within the relationship. At the same time, communication provides feedback and discloses feelings. There is an honest sharing of what each person experiences.

Effective communication is characterized by the ability to express *and* to empathize. By expressing your feelings you will learn to understand your own emotions and to express them in ways that will not cause you anxiety, conflict, or hostility. You will learn to focus on developing respect, understanding, cooperation, and the open sharing of your feelings with your partner. By empathizing, you will understand the emotional and psychological needs of your partner and be better able to communicate to him or her that you *do* understand.

Thoughts, feelings, and behaviors are the basic elements that are combined to create the marriage relationship or system. By focusing on these elements, you can create a mutually satisfying marriage; however, if you only *think* to yourself that you love your spouse very much, and don't even look up or move to kiss or hug your partner when he or she leaves or returns from work, you are being incongruent, feeling or thinking one way and acting another. Successful couples are aligned and think, feel, and act congruently. Feelings of love and caring are shared through words and deeds. Partners show they care through nonverbal gestures such as smiles, pats, and eye contact; through verbal statements such as "I love you," "I like it when . . . ," "I enjoy being with you"; and through thoughtful acts such as phone calls, love notes, surprise dates, or gifts.

Not knowing how to maintain or keep a relationship growing is one reason for a failing marriage. Here are four others:

1. *Lack of skills.* Partners often lack appropriate sharing and problem-solving skills, such as communication, conflict resolution, and encouragement. Many people also suffer from the belief that two people "fall in love," which tends to communicate that the individual has no control over his or her marital fate. This is a myth. Love is a product of very specific skills, attitudes, and ways of relating that are acquired, not inherited, and therefore can be taught and learned.

2. *Unrealistic expectations.* We were raised on the myth that the happy couple lives happily ever after. This created the belief that love happens to people; in reality, *love is a product of two people who treat each other in a loving manner.* It is important for couples to exhibit the following loving behaviors in order to create love:

- Make time on a daily basis for your partner.
- Show respect for your partner by attending and listening to what he or she says.
- Speak to your partner in an encouraging manner and provide positive support and feedback.
- Communicate feelings in a congruent fashion.
- Listen and send messages clearly.
- Make loving choices.
- Use skills that process rather than suppress anger.
- Resolve conflicts using healthy skills.
- Reserve quality time for fun each week with your partner.
- Meet on a weekly basis to discuss issues surrounding your marriage.

For any marriage to be effective, more realistic expectations about responsibilities are needed. Unrealistic expectations leave both partners feeling that they are *entitled* or it is *their right* to special treatment without having to return the same.

3. *Lack of respect.* It has often been illustrated how partners do and say things to each other that they would never do or say to anyone else. This behavior is an asset when it is applied to some of the special, intimate areas of marriage but is a real problem when it involves negative actions (e.g., talking over your spouse, answering for him or her, or not asking for his or her opinion; demanding rather than asking for something; taking a thoughtful act for granted rather than saying thank you). Respect is the single most important ingredient in a marriage. You

must value your partner and want to understand and experience his or her world. Without respect, no union or relationship is possible.

Marriages are run under the principle of quid pro quo. Literally this means "something for something." A marriage is balanced like a bank account. You make deposits and withdrawals. A system needs balance. An effective and satisfying marriage involves making deposits and receiving returns. Every couple needs to decide the rights and duties of each spouse.

4. *Forgetting positive attitudes and courage.* In most relationships, we tend to remember the negative, or what's wrong, and forget the positive, or what's working. Healthy relationships are just the opposite; they encourage the positive and caring acts of partnership. This positive attitude is contagious and carries over into all our dealings with one another. Quite simply, we like to be around positive people because they make us feel better.

Small Steps = Big Results

This book will show you how to integrate positive behaviors into your daily routines and life-style. You will learn how to do this through specific instructions that we have used with thousands of couples in private therapy with a great deal of success and by filling out questionnaires. *A word of caution:* The tasks and exercises in this book may seem simple. Don't be deceived by their simplicity. These exercises are remarkably effective strategies for initiating the changes you need to adjust, maintain, and sustain your marriage. You'll be surprised at how easy it can be to turn a difficult marital situation into one that is mutually satisfying.

These exercises will also work on specific issues in your relationship to bring about constructive changes. If your relationship changes profoundly after following our instructions, and neither you nor your spouse is able to explain what has happened or exactly why, don't be concerned. You do not need to have a thorough intellectual understanding of the processes; you need only appreciate and enjoy the results.

The exercises in *Taking Time for Love* have been designed to stop the problems discussed above from ruining your marriage. Most people want a better marriage but are not willing or able to make *major* concessions or changes. They will make some small changes, however, and these small changes, if properly executed, can produce large results—that is what this book is all about. We'll show you that the odds of positive change increase if the goal is reasonably small and clearly stated. Small changes also help us overcome fear. Our fears (and we all have them) have a tendency to make us keep to ourselves, and this keeps us apart in our relationships. Most of us have feelings of inferiority, and we are afraid our partner will find out just how unworthy we feel. Will Durant said, "Our instincts were formed during a thousand centuries of insecurity." We will show you that you have within yourself the power and/or ability to rise above your inheritance if you move slowly and take small steps.

This book, if used as suggested, will increase your rate

of daily, positive exchanges with your partner. It will produce a prompt, immediate, and beneficial effect. You and your spouse will both learn that change is possible, as you learn to express *(and not just verbalize)* your caring. It is much more satisfying to respond to the positive actions of your partner than to simply hear empty words. Hearing your spouse say "I love you" as he or she bolts out the door is just not as convincing as hearing your spouse say the same words as he or she holds you close and looks into your eyes. This expression of caring is a change that will help to maintain your relationship and to keep it growing.

In our marriage enrichment program, *TIME: Training in Marriage Enrichment* (Dinkmeyer and Carlson, 1984), we identified some helpful principles for change. We have adapted them here to provide you with the ingredients necessary for you to benefit most from the suggestions in this book.

1. *Commitment to change is the first step in enriching a marriage.* All change begins within each of you. Begin by understanding what your role in the marriage has been and what you can do to make it different. Be patient in your growth and allow for different rates of change. Too many people blame their partners for the failure of their relationship because they do not feel that they are a part of the problem and, therefore, do not know their role as part of the solution. Remember: Both partners are equally involved in creating the outcome of their marriage. What is your role and responsibilities? What can you do differently?

2. *Developing and maintaining a good marital relationship requires a time commitment.* For your marriage relationship to succeed, you must make it an important time priority now and in the future. Ask yourself these questions: How much time did you spend with each other during courtship? How much time do you spend with each other now? Do you spend *quality* time with each other on a daily basis?

3. *Specific problem-solving skills that are essential to a healthy marriage can be learned—it's never too late.* By understanding how a marriage works and the skills necessary for building a successful marriage, you will also learn, develop, and use the skills that create a positive, rewarding relationship. Unfortunately, many people believe that their marriage would be better if only the problems could be removed. Problems do not go away. Satisfied couples have the same problems as unsatisfied couples; the difference is that satisfied couples possess the skills to resolve problems quickly with minimal disruption to daily life. Think about skills you can develop further. What skills do you already have?

4. *Feelings of love and caring that have diminished or disappeared often return when behavior changes.* Romantic feelings, intimacy, and love often diminish over time in a marriage relationship. When feelings are not expressed on a regular basis, many couples believe that the relationship is over. This need not be the case. A change in feelings may mean that you and your partner are not being mutually encouraged in the marriage and that the relationship deserves a higher priority. It is important at such times to act *as if* all were well. By acting *as if* your

relationship is the intimate, satisfying relationship you desire, new behaviors and feelings can be established. Think about the changes needed in your relationship. Can you act as if they have already occurred?

5. *Small changes are very important because they bring about big changes.* A happier relationship results from many small changes over a period of time. Even though both you and your partner are committed to change, there may be times when unwanted patterns reappear. This does not mean that the new skills you are learning are not working in your marriage. Periodic regression to old ways of relating is normal and predictable. Do not become overconcerned. Be patient and continue to focus on the positive relationship you desire; these times of testing will pass.

Marriage Assessment

Marriage Assessment is a structured opportunity to tell the truth to yourself about the kind of marital relationship you have. This is not a test, there are no trick questions, and the answers will have meaning only for you.

Here's how it works. By the end of this exercise you will have answered fifty questions and filled in on the graph on page 16 a picture of how you see your marriage. The closer the shading comes to covering the entire circle, the higher your evaluation of your relationship is. The areas with the least shading are those you feel need to be improved. The purpose of the shading in the circle is to create a visual representation or shape. Remember: This shape is not what your marriage is; rather, it is a picture of what you *think* your marriage is. To begin, read the following statements and give yourself points for each one accordingly:

5 = This statement is always or almost always true of me.

4 = This statement is often true of me.

3 = This statement is sometimes, about half, true of me.

2 = This statement is seldom true of me.

1 = This statement is never or almost never true of me.

Answer the following questions:

A. *Thoughts*

_____ 1. I think of my partner with positive thoughts.

_____ 2. I respect my partner's decisions and choices.

_____ 3. I am proud of my partner and can accept him/her as he/she is.

_____ 4. I am able to change my negative thoughts into positive ones.

_____ 5. I take responsibility for the state of my marriage.

_____ 6. I believe satisfaction is more important than perfection.

_____ 7. I am able to choose my thoughts instead of merely reacting.

_____ 8. I am able to identify many ideas, beliefs, feelings, and goals that are similar to my partner's.

_____ 9. I am able to affirm myself and I do so each day. I use positive self-talk.

_____ 10. I am able to identify and talk back to my negative thoughts.

_____ Total/Part A

B. Feelings

_____ 1. I am in charge and take responsibility for my feelings.

_____ 2. I am empathetic and understand my partner's feelings.

_____ 3. I am able to change my feelings to see the positive in a situation.

_____ 4. I am able to process anger effectively with my partner.

_____ 5. I speak my feelings honestly and say what I feel to my partner.

_____ 6. I use "I" messages whenever appropriate, sharing my feelings directly, instead of using "you" messages that blame my spouse.

_____ 7. I share my feelings on a regular basis with my partner.

_____ 8. I am able to focus on feelings of love.

_____ 9. I can express feelings with words, touch, or in writing to my partner.

_____ 10. I can create positive feelings whenever I choose.

_____ Total/Part B

C. Behavior

_____ 1. I encourage my partner each day.

_____ 2. I can identify behaviors in myself and my partner that please me.

_____ 3. I hug my partner daily.

_____ 4. I practice daily encouragement meetings with my partner.

_____ 5. I show my appreciation for my partner daily.

_____ 6. I often leave "I love you" notes and other thoughtful gifts.

_____ 7. I communicate nonverbally in positive ways to my partner.

_____ 8. I take time each day to value myself.

_____ 9. I have fun and enjoyment when I'm with my partner.

_____ 10. I plan a surprise for my partner at least once each month.

_____ Total/Part C

D. System

_____ 1. I spend ten minutes each day in dialogue with my partner.

_____ 2. I can resolve conflict with my partner in a manner that is mutually satisfying.

_____ 3. I show respect to my partner.

_____ 4. I pinpoint the real issues in our conflicts.

_____ 5. I work through conflicts with my partner.

_____ 6. I participate mutually in problem solving with my partner.

_____ 7. I spend quality time with my partner.

_____ 8. I hold a weekly marriage meeting with my partner.

_____ 9. I can identify ten ways my partner can show he/she cares for me.

_____ 10. I express laughter and humor daily.

_____   Total/Part D

E. Intimacy

_____   1. I am well informed on sexuality and lovemaking.

_____   2. I feel comfortable touching and being touched by my partner.

_____   3. I feel comfortable discussing sex with my partner.

_____   4. I regularly make time for sex and lovemaking.

_____   5. I continue to "court" my partner.

_____   6. I regularly have sexual fantasies and communicate them to my partner.

_____   7. I feel comfortable saying no occasionally to my partner's request for sex.

_____   8. I avoid falling into rigid and/or boring sexual routines.

_____   9. I take responsibility for my own sexual pleasure.

_____ 10. I feel fit and sexy.

_____   Total/Part E

When you have finished, add up your point totals for each section. Fifty points are possible in each section. Next, create a marriage profile by shading in the circle on page 16 to the appropriate total point level. Examine your perception of your marriage on the chart. You can see which of the five areas is your strong point and which ones are your work areas. Compare your marriage profile with your partner's. In what areas do you complement each other? In what areas are you similar?

Each of the following chapters pertains to one of the slices of the pie. Work with the exercises in each section, to either make a strong area stronger or improve an area.

Marriage Profile Graph

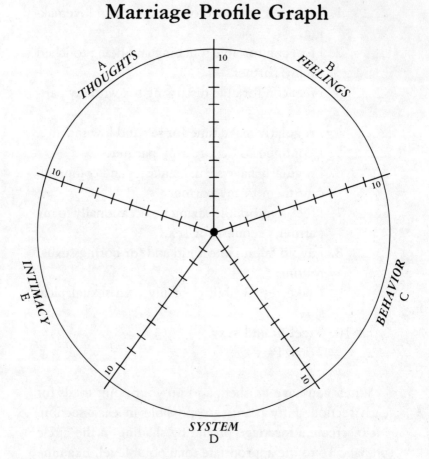

·2·

Time for Loving Thoughts

How you think about your marriage often influences how you experience your marriage. People who think about marriage as a valuable, positive institution often create the atmosphere for this type of marriage. Those who think of marriage as a struggle, battle, or an obligation often have an unsatisfying experience.

Planned interventions that change your thinking have definite effects on how you feel and act. For example, in a crowded theater, a woman suddenly stands up, slaps the face of the man next to her, and hurries down the aisle to an exit. Each person watching the event reacts in his or her own special way. One woman is frightened. A teenager is angry. A middle-age man becomes depressed. A social worker feels a pleasurable excitement.

Why did the same event trigger very different feelings throughout the audience? The answer can be found by examining the thoughts of each observer. The fearful woman thought, "He's going to go after her when they get home, and then she's really going to get it." She

17

imagined the details and recalled the times when she had been physically abused. The angry teenager thought, "He just wanted a kiss, and she humiliated him. The poor guy, she must really be a bitch." The middle-age man thought, "Now he's lost her, and he'll never get her back." He could see his ex-wife's face set in angry lines. The social worker felt a delicious pleasure as she thought, "Serves him right. What a strong woman! I wish some timid women I know had seen that."

In each case, the observer's feeling was a consequence of his or her thoughts. The event was interpreted, judged, and labeled in such a way that a special feeling was inevitable. We are constantly describing the world to ourselves, giving a label to each event or each experience. We judge events as good or bad, painful or pleasurable. We also predict whether they will bring danger or relative safety. These labels and judgments, fashioned from the unending dialogue we all have with ourselves, color all our experiences with private meaning.

The following exercises have been created to help you change any unhealthy thoughts about your marriage into more positive and satisfying thoughts by helping to modify your internal dialogue.

Loving Thought #1: Respect

Recent research indicates that respect and positive regard are the key ingredients of a healthy marriage. Respect involves giving your partner the benefit of the doubt, respecting his or her decisions and choices. It involves a noncritical acceptance. Thinking of your partner in positive ways and describing your partner's strengths are important ingredients of a healthy marriage.

In a healthy marriage, partners are able to identify and quickly describe why they respect each other. For example, when Bill comes home late from the office and isn't able to call, Cheryl respects him and supports his efforts, and she says, "I'm really glad you're home and appreciate how hard you're working for our family." Ron is waiting fifteen minutes for Sue to prepare for their evening out. Even though they're going to be late, when she appears, he says, "I really like the way you look and appreciate how you take the time to look good for me and make a good impression on others."

Take one minute and see how many different ways you can fill in the following statement about your partner:

"I respect you for _____."

For example, you may respond, "I respect you for *understanding my need to work late,*" "I respect you for *telling me the truth, even though I might not want to hear it,*" "I respect you for *sharing in household work,*" or "I respect you for *supporting my efforts.*"

Each day, write three or more statements and try to see how many different positive responses you can generate from your knowledge of your partner.

What about your partner makes you proud? Write your answers on cards and surprise your partner by hiding them in special places (for example: "I am proud of you, Roger, because of the firm yet kind way you treat others" or "I am proud of you, Sandy, because of the way you can manage so many things at the same time").

Try the following brief exercise to generate increased respect in your marriage:

1. Choose a current problem that you and your partner see as an issue in your relationship. Choose one that you do not agree on.

2. Imagine listening to your partner's point of view with alert interest. Imagine that you are seeing this problem through your partner's eyes. Write in your own words how you believe your partner sees this issue.

3. Give your essay to your partner.

4. Have your partner return it, indicating how accurate you are.

5. Do this with many different issues one at a time.

Loving Thought #2: Changing Negative to Positive Thoughts

Stereotyped thinking and rigid ideas about what a wife or a husband should be and do tend to get in the way of an effective and growing marriage. Couples involved in growing marriages are continually looking for and changing these negative, growth-inhibiting thoughts and replacing them with different positive thoughts.

Try this exercise: Identify a stereotyped thought that you have (e.g., "My wife must always be romantic") and replace it with a positive thought. Each day for the next week, identify one stereotyped thought that you can change.

Often in marriage we have many vague and negative gripes about our partners. As part of this exercise, try to turn these negative gripes into specific requests for positive change. This process involves using "I messages," which are more positive than "you messages." (This procedure is discussed fully in chapter 3.) If possible, do this exercise with your partner and discuss it as you go.

Negative or Vague	*becomes*	*Specific and Positive*
You are lazy.		I would like you to help with the housecleaning.
You never listen.		I would like you to look at me when I talk.

Now take your own gripes and write them into specific and positive requests. Discuss them with each other.

Negative or Vague	*becomes*	*Specific and Positive*
You're immature.		_____
You're too soft with the kids.		_____
You're a show-off.		_____
You're always jealous.		_____
You don't care how I feel.		_____
You don't want me sexually.		_____

If you have trouble identifying a rigid thought, ask your partner to help you recognize those that you may not be aware of. One of our clients, Bob, believed that his wife, Jane, only looked good when she was dressed up, so he never said positive things to her except when they were dressed formally. By using this exercise and talking with Jane, he updated his thinking to see the positive in how she looked at all times, whether in a formal or an informal setting. Sally believed that the only way to solve problems was to talk them out before bedtime and never go to bed with a problem unsolved. By using this exercise she updated her thinking to believe that one way to solve problems is to resolve everything before bedtime, but it is not the only way. Some problems are better left until the next day.

By learning to change your thoughts and describing your partner's strengths and seeing your partner more positively, you will become more attracted to him or her and your relationship will improve.

Loving Thought #3: Responsibility to Change

Either partner can *choose* to make his or her marriage different once he or she is willing to take responsibility for change. We change when we can visualize our future. Having a clear thought or picture can motivate and guide us so that the type of marriage we eventually want can become a reality. Setting yourself on a path to achieve your future goals will dictate how you should act in certain situations in the present.

For example, if you have negative thoughts about the future of your marriage, you will be compelled to act in ways that are likely to produce negative results. On the other hand, positive thoughts will compel you to behave in ways that will make your marriage more satisfying.

The purpose of the following exercise is to help you to develop goals that will create healthy thoughts and constructive marital behavior. Always keep in mind the old Chinese proverb, "If you don't change your direction, you will end up where you're headed."

Now, read through steps 1 and 2 of the following exercise before you begin step 3:

Step 1: Imagine you and your partner in one year, five years, and ten years. Construct a mental picture or visual representation of yourself at each date. Picture what you want your life to be like at each stage.

Step 2: Take a deep breath and become aware of the sensations and feelings that you have at each of these milestones.

Step 3: Become aware of what you should be doing now in order to reach the future that you have pictured. List five specific behaviors and activities that you need to exercise in order to meet your goals and five behaviors and activities that you need to avoid.

A. Things Worth Doing to Lead You to Your Future Goals

_____

_____

_____

_____

_____

B. Things Worth Avoiding Because They Will Lead You Away from Your Future Goals

_____

_____

_____

_____

_____

_____

Loving Thought #4: Beliefs

A belief is your own opinion about something. It is what you think or accept to be true. In an effective and healthy marriage, it is necessary for both partners to periodically update their beliefs with regard to sex, beauty, finances, and so on.

Differences in beliefs abound in relationships. For example, Julie knows she is loved when David hangs on her every word and always wants to be with her. On the other hand, David knows that he is loved when Julie does not bother him with fawning attention, and he is most happy to see her off on her own. In marriage, it is often necessary to learn to realize that both conditions are true. A belief in only one viewpoint results in problems.

Many marriages operate on false beliefs, and a marriage that operates this way is bound to fail. Don't let this happen to you. Read the following "marital myths" with your partner and discuss how adherence to them would limit the potential of a marriage.

- If you feel you only *like* your partner now, you have fallen out of love.
- If you and your partner really love each other, you will spend all your time together.
- If you and your partner really love each other, you will automatically know how the other thinks and feels.
- If you and your partner really love each other, you will automatically communicate well.
- If the relationship is in trouble, usually one of the partners is to blame (usually the other partner).
- If you and your partner love each other, good sex comes naturally.
- Arguments clear the air and enable you to make up and feel good.
- An argument can end only by one partner giving in and admitting that he or she is wrong.
- If your partner feels love for someone else, he/she must feel less love for you.
- If your partner feels sexually attracted to someone else, he/she must feel less attracted to you.
- If you want your partner to do something, nagging is the best way to get him or her to do it. If you want your partner to stop nagging, give in.

Couples share many of the same beliefs and yet have some unique ones. In the exercise that follows, identify beliefs that you need to modify in order to have a healthy marriage.

In this example, one couple reveals their feelings about partner's expressing emotion.

Belief	*Healthier Belief*
A real man must not cry or express emotions to his partner.	To make a marriage work both partners need to express emotions to each other.

1. Write a belief that you have about sex.

Belief	*Healthier Belief*
_____	_____
_____	_____
_____	_____
_____	_____

2. Write a belief that you have about beauty.

Belief	*Healthier Belief*
_____	_____
_____	_____
_____	_____
_____	_____

3. Write a belief that you have about financé.

Belief	*Healthier Belief*
_____	_____
_____	_____
_____	_____
_____	_____

Loving Thought #5:
Perfection Versus Satisfaction

"If we really love each other we will *never* fight or argue."

"Sex must be great *every* time."

It is important for couples to learn how to create satisfaction, not perfection, in marriage. Couples need to learn how to develop and create what they really want in their marriage. All-or-nothing thinking often gives rise to perfectionism, which does not lead to a happy marriage. Look around and ask yourself how many things in the world can be broken down into all-or-nothing categories. Are the walls around you *totally* clean, or do they have some dirt? Does your favorite athlete *always* perform perfectly? Do you know anyone who is totally calm and confident *all the time?* Everything can be improved if you look at it critically enough: every person, every idea, every work of art, every experience. It is helpful to learn to recognize this all-or-nothing "perfectionist" thinking, especially as it applies to your marriage, because this type of thinking destroys relationships.

If you are a perfectionist, you may find it hard to believe that you can enjoy life to the maximum or find happiness without aiming for perfection. You can put this notion to a test. On a piece of paper, list a wide range of activities, (e.g., mowing the lawn, preparing a meal, writing a report for work). In column one record the *actual* satisfaction you get from each activity by scoring it from 0 to 100 percent. In column two estimate how perfectly you do each activity, again using a scale of zero to 100 percent.

Taking Time for Love

Activity	Actual Satisfaction 0% (none)–100% (complete)	Estimated Degree of Perfection 0% (none)–100% (perfect)
Mowing the lawn	80	60
Preparing a meal	75	40
Report writing	50	50

Use the following categories in addition to the ones you choose: sex, paying the bills, disciplining children, playing your favorite sport.

Activity	Actual Satisfaction 0% (none)–100% (complete)	Estimated Degree of Perfection 0% (none)–100% (perfect)
Sex	_____	_____
Paying the bills	_____	_____
Disciplining children	_____	_____
Favorite sport	_____	_____

Now add up each column and compare the difference. This exercise should help you realize that satisfaction and perfection are not the same, that we are in fact satisfied with much less than we actually believe will be enough.

Loving Thought #6: Acting, Not Reacting

It is Saturday night and you are looking forward to a romance-filled evening and your partner says "I just want to go to sleep." Automatically you react. What are your thoughts? "He/she can't do this to me," "Maybe tomorrow night," "It's not fair . . ." Each of us responds automatically to situations even before we have all the facts. The purpose of the exercise that follows is to determine if your automatic responses are building a healthy relationship or tearing you apart.

Hearing your automatic thoughts is the first step in gaining control. The automatic thoughts that cause harm can be identified because they almost always precede a constantly painful emotion. To identify the automatic thoughts that are causing continued painful feelings, try to recall the feelings you had just prior to the start of the emotion and those that accompany the sustained emotion. You can think of the process as listening in on an intercom. The intercom is always on, even while you are conversing with others and going about your life. You are functioning in the world, and you are talking to yourself at the same time. Listen in on the intercom of your internal dialogue and hear what you are telling yourself. The automatic thoughts are assigning private meanings to the things that happen to you. They are making judgments and interpretations of your experience. These thoughts are often lightning fast and very difficult to catch. They flash on as a great mental image or telegraph a single word. Use the following methods to cope with these thoughts:

• Reconstruct a problem situation; go over it in your imagination until the painful emotion begins to emerge. What are you thinking as the emotion comes up? Replay your thoughts in slow motion. Look at your internal dialogue frame by frame. Notice the millisecond it takes to say "I can't stand it" or the half-second image of a terrifying event. Notice how you internally describe and interpret the actions of others: "She's bored," "He's putting me down."

• Stretch out the shorthand statement into the original sentence from which it was extracted. Feeling tired is really "I'm not attracted to you." Crazy means "I feel like I'm losing control, and that must mean I'm going crazy. My friends will reject me." Hearing the shorthand isn't enough. It is necessary to listen to the entire syllogism in order to understand the distorted logic from which your painful emotions bloom.

To appreciate the power of your automatic thoughts and the part they play in your emotional life, make your own "Thoughts Diary." Make a notation each time you experience an unpleasant emotion. Include everything you tell yourself to keep the emotion going.

THOUGHTS DIARY

Automatic Thought

Time   _____

Emotion   _____

Situation   _____

How true now _____

How true at bedtime _____

Loving Thought #7:
Learning to Reframe and Find the Positive

"It's not the things themselves which trouble us,
but the opinions that we have about these things."

Epictetus

The same situation can be viewed many different ways. How we view a situation will depend on what it means to us and how we react. Learning to see a problem from an alternative viewpoint is often a way to reduce or eliminate it. When you have trouble with your partner and relationship you often think the worst has occurred. It is possible, however, to reframe and to view the situation from a more positive viewpoint. Frank says, "Things are awful with my wife. She never listens to me, and all she does is complain. I decided just to stop paying any attention to her when she complains. Maybe she'll get the idea." How might Frank see this situation differently?

When we become aware of perceptual alternatives, of the variety of ways we have of giving meaning to a specific event, we are more in control of our options. We are able to choose how to interpret an event and how to behave. For example, Frank might view his wife as troubled and overwhelmed by her work and see her complaining as a request for understanding and involvement. He may also view it as a sign of nervousness by noticing that whenever his wife becomes upset and nervous she begins to complain in a rapid-fire fashion.

Events may be seen in a discouraging or an encouraging way. Ron calls Mary and says he won't be home until late and will miss their dinner date because he has to complete a report. Mary might respond in an encouraging way and say, "I really like the way you're so responsible. I know I can always count on you, Ron." Or, even though she has all the facts, she may view things in a discouraging manner and say, "What are you doing, got a date? Don't you think I'm important?" In the following exercises, create the situation described and an encouraging perceptual alternative.

1. Think of the last time you felt your partner treated you unfairly. Recall why you felt you were unfairly treated and develop ways of seeing the situation differently.

2. Think of a situation in which you felt embarrassed, humiliated, or snubbed by your partner. How else could you have viewed it?

3. Think of a situation that occurred today; reframe it in a positive manner.

Loving Thought #8: Things You Have in Common

In our society, we often focus on what's wrong or what isn't working right. In a marital relationship, if you continue to focus on what goes wrong and what isn't working for you, you often forget why you and your partner are together and the ideas, beliefs, feelings, and goals you share.

Take one minute to identify what you have in common with your partner. Do this three different times today and identify as many similarities as you can. Share your list with your partner. Have your partner share his or her list with you.

Things We Have in Common
- We enjoy watching plays.
- We care about children.
- We feel sorry for less fortunate people.
- We worship in the same way.
- We like similar jokes.
- We like to swim.
- We enjoy traveling together.
-
-
-
-

Loving Thought #9: Agreements

Following on Loving Thought # 8, we often lose track of the many things that we agree on with our partners. Today, complete the same assignment that you did for Loving Thought # 8, but this time identify the areas on which you and your partner agree. Look for agreement in feelings, behavior, values, and attitudes.

Things We Agree On
- We agree that children should be active in both sports and music.
- We agree that we each need to have our own friends.
- We agree that anger will be expressed within twenty-four hours.
- We agree to take turns asking each other for a date.
-
-
-
-

Loving Thought #10: Marital Self-Talk

Learning the value of positive thinking and self-encouragement and practicing these techniques can greatly help a relationship. By encouraging yourself, you increase your sense of personal worth. To be a resource to others, you must develop self-esteem. Your self-esteem will grow as you learn to identify, verbalize, and act on your personal strengths. Get rid of your fear of failure by not embracing it, holding on to it, or using it as an excuse to avoid positive movement. Learn to discover your hidden potential. Compliment yourself. Be sure the messages you are giving yourself are positive messages: "I am a good friend," "People like me," "My opinion is important," or "Others count on me."*

Each day, pick one of the seven phrases listed below and repeat it ten times either silently or aloud to yourself. Before beginning the exercise, relax and concentrate fully on the phrase. Sit in a comfortable location and position. Close your eyes and take four long, slow breaths before beginning.

1. I feel confident in my ability, and I will act in a confident manner. I am confident that I can handle any situation that confronts me in a way that allows me to reach my goal.

2. I am relaxed and patient. I am in no hurry. There is lots and lots of time. When I relax, I have more patience. When I am patient with myself, I do all things better and like myself more.

3. I relate with others in a friendly and confident fashion. I express my feelings, ideas, and opinions freely but tactfully. I meet new people with ease and confidence. I encourage others in a free and sincere fashion.

4. I work hard to understand others. I listen closely and choose words that let them know I understand.

*Many couples have found that the "self-encouragement" section of our audio-tape *Time to Relax and Imagine* is an excellent method of developing positive self-messages. The audiotape is available form American Guidance Service, Circle Pines, MN 55014; tel.: (800) 328–2560.

5. I work hard and I persist in my efforts to reach my goals. I realize there are things that I cannot control. In particular, I cannot control other people. Other people can cause a temporary setback in my progress toward my goal. I recognize it for what it is, only a temporary setback.

6. I accept my partner. I notice my partner's good qualities. I am more and more aware of qualities in my partner that are pleasing to me. I am thinking of these qualities now.

7. I accept responsibility for the success of my marriage. I know that what I do today makes a difference between a happy and an unhappy marriage.

Loving Thought #11: Talking Back to Negative Thoughts

Write down the negative thought that goes through your mind when you are upset. What are you telling yourself? Are you being illogical or harsh? Draw a line down the middle of a piece of paper. In one column write your negative thoughts: "I'm not a good lover," "I'm no good," "I'm a loser," or "I'll never get close to anyone." In the other column write realistic or positive thoughts: "I'm a good lover and getting better," "I'm good at many things," "I have the courage to be imperfect," or "I'm growing more confident in relationships each day." Talk back to these thoughts; pretend a friend was saying these things to you. Don't do this exercise in your head. You must write down your thoughts and responses.

Negative Thought

*Talk Back with a Positive
Thought*

_____   _____

_____   _____

_____   _____

_____   _____

_____   _____

Loving Thought #12: Changing Rituals

Routines quickly develop in marriage relationships.
They often develop without conscious forethought or
even mutual discussion and agreement. The routines
eventually become boundaries that determine what can
and cannot happen.

Imagine how your marriage would be different if it
moved beyond its present boundaries. Think of five ways
you can change the boundaries. Take one time segment
and make it happen. For example, "I usually get up and
prepare my own breakfast and Susan does the same. Tomorrow I plan to make something for her and take it to
her in the bedroom. It won't take long and I know she'll
appreciate the thought."

Breakfast   _____
Dinner   _____
Evening Hours   _____
Bedtime   _____
Weekend   _____

Loving Thought #13: Dealing with Expectations

You have many expectations of your partner in marriage. Some are well thought out and agreed to; others are more subtle and possibly troublesome. Your expectations come largely from your family of origin. How you were raised represents the life-style and rules for living with which you are most comfortable and familiar. You internalize the existence and expect that your marriage will be exactly like the experiences you enjoyed and different from those that were less satisfying. Unfortunately, you seldom verbalize these goals or act in a different fashion.

This situation becomes complicated when two family-of-origin systems are merged. Some areas of agreement certainly occur or a marriage would be unlikely; however, many areas are left unclear and unspoken. Each partner has a picture of and thoughts about the partner he/she wants; these pictures become expectations, many of which are never verbalized and may actually be unhealthy or impossible.

List several expectations that you have of your partner. For example, he/she should be more appreciative, more loving, more attentive, more cheerful, more prompt, more understanding, and so on. Examine each expectation. Rethink and reframe using the skills discussed in Loving Thought #7 (page 31).

Expectation	*Rethink*
More appreciative	I need to be more appreciative.
More loving	I need to communicate how I want to be loved.

Before you go out together, practice what you may say to your partner to indicate your enjoyment: "I'm having a great time, darling. Let's do this again soon" or "This is fabulous. I had forgotten what great fun this could be." Planning ahead so that you know what you will say will help you avoid slipping into statements that might imply criticism or, even worse, saying nothing at all. If you are not used to making nice statements to your partner, it will not happen spontaneously; therefore, rehearse the compliments you may make to your partner in order to break this negative cycle and express the pleasure that you truly feel. At the same time, think ahead about how *you* will respond to a pleasant or complimentary statement made by your partner: "It was really nice of you to say that" or "I'm really glad that you told me how much you are enjoying yourself."

Time for Loving Feelings

How a person feels about his or her marriage often influences the relationship within the marriage. An individual who has positive feelings toward his or her partner often produces a positive relationship. Feelings are not just emotions that happen to you. Feelings are reactions you choose to have. For example, when your partner is late you can choose to feel angry, concerned, worried, or happy that he or she is with you now. It is possible to make yourself feel any way you choose to feel. Emotions are a choice, not a condition of life. In chapter 2 we discussed how it is possible to control thoughts. Feelings often come from thoughts; therefore, as you control your thoughts, you are also able to control your feelings.

A feeling is a physical reaction to a thought. If you cry or blush or increase your heartbeat, you first have a signal from your thinking center. Every feeling that you have is preceded by a thought, and without a thought you can have no feelings. If you control your thoughts and your feelings come from your thoughts, then you are capable of controlling your own feelings. You can control your feelings by working on the thoughts that precede them. Simply put, you may *believe* that your partner makes you unhappy, or that your marriage makes you unhappy— but that is not accurate. You make yourself feel unhappy because of the thoughts that you have about your partner or your marriage. To become a loving, cooperative partner involves learning to think and feel differently.

We have all grown up with input that tells us to suppress our feelings and emotions. It is because of this conditioning that we haven't allowed ourselves to experience our emotions and feelings. As a matter of fact, most of us do not even know what it means to fully experience our emotions and feelings. Full experience requires that we not blame anybody else for our feelings. The statements in the column on the left are examples of how we avoid taking responsibility for our feelings; those in the column on the right are examples of how we should take responsibility for our feelings.

Blaming Others	*Taking Responsibility for Our Own Feelings*
You hurt my feelings.	I hurt my feelings because of the things I told myself about your reaction to me.
You make me feel bad.	I make myself feel bad.
I can't help the way I feel.	I can help the way I feel because I've chosen to be upset.

I just feel angry. Don't ask me to explain.	I've decided to be angry because I can usually manipulate others with my anger, since they think I control them.
He makes me sick.	I make myself sick.
You're embarrassing me.	I'm embarrassing myself.
She really turns me on.	I turn myself on whenever I'm near her.
He made a fool of me in public.	I made myself feel foolish by taking your opinions of me more seriously than my own and believing that others would do the same.

The list in the left-hand column is potentially endless and each saying conveys the message that you are not responsible for how you feel; however, as we have seen, the list can be rewritten so that it is accurate. The contrasting messages in the right-hand column reflect the fact that this person is now in charge and recognizes that his or her feelings come from thoughts.

The message is that you are responsible for how you feel. If you feel what you think, then you can learn to think differently about anything, if you decide to do so. You might ask yourself if there is a payoff in being unhappy, down, or hurt. Use the exercises that follow to begin to examine in more detail your feelings and how to change them to more appropriate feelings.

Loving Feeling #1: Understanding Your Partner's Feelings

Learning to be empathetic and to understand your partner's feelings is important for maintaining a happy, healthy relationship. Research indicates that people have problems communicating with one another. The basic skill for effective communication is empathy, or understanding how others feel and making clear to them that you understand how they feel. Although we hope that husbands and wives are perhaps best at putting themselves in their partner's position, research indicates that they are often worse than others, not only in terms of their ability to understand one another but also in terms of the amount of time that they spend together. Research indicates that the average American couple spends only a few minutes each week communicating.

It is very important to understand your partner's feelings. When we talk to another person in any relationship, we request one of five things: action, information, inappropriate interaction, understanding and involvement. And more often than not, the requests that are made to us are for understanding and involvement. If you are not empathetic, you will not be able to demonstrate your understanding and the extent of your involvement with your partner. A marriage cannot exist without empathy.

As an exercise, ask yourself on three different occasions today how your partner feels at the moment. Allow one minute to answer. On a piece of paper, note the time and write what you think your partner is doing and how he/she feels at that moment. At the end of the day, show your list to your partner and ask your spouse to confirm how he or she was feeling. This exercise will help you to identify your level of empathy.

As an optional activity, focus on how you wish you were feeling now about your partner. Think of the feelings that you wish you were feeling now, the feelings that you would be having if your marriage was the way you want it to be. How would you be feeling at this moment? For example, "I would feel excited by the anticipation of being together tonight" or "I would be confident that he/she is thinking about the best interests of both of us."

The following exercise is a nonthreatening way to practice empathy. Watch a TV show you hate, one you normally wouldn't be caught dead watching. If you normally watch game shows, pick a serious drama. If you normally watch only news, tune in some cartoons. If you prefer comedies, watch a TV preacher or a crime show or a soap opera. Watch and listen carefully. Every time you feel irritated, disgusted, bored, or embarrassed, set your feelings aside and refocus your attention. Say to yourself, "I notice I'm feeling very irritated by this. That's okay, but it's not what I'm interested in right now. I can set the irritation aside and just observe for a while without judging." Suspend your value judgments for a time and imagine why the faithful fans of the show watch it. What do they get out of it? Do they watch for excitement, enlightenment, diversion, escape, identification with the characters, or confirmation of their prejudices? Try to understand the attractive features of this show and what kind of person likes it. When you arrive at an empathetic understanding, switch to another show you do not like and try again. Remember, you don't have to approve of what you see—just see it clearly and understand its attractions. The goal of this exercise isn't to expand or corrupt your viewing tastes. The purpose is to provide a safe, nonthreatening situation in which you can practice setting aside your snap judgments and gain an insight into a point of view you would ordinarily dismiss out of hand.

Loving Feeling #2: Changing Negative Feelings into Positive Feelings

Alfred Adler, the renowned Viennese psychiatrist, once stated that everything can be something else. Adler used this idea to help others to learn to *reframe* situations so that they would look and feel differently. Each partner may view the same event or situation differently but accurately. For example, Bill is very happy about the new car, while Mary worries whether they can afford the payments. Sally looks forward with excitement and glee to a planned night in the bedroom, while Norm views it as a dreaded obligation. The partners' feelings may vary in the same situation.

By understanding that it is possible to see the same

situation from different perspectives, couples can move to healthier, more loving feelings. In this exercise, we will look at a four-step process for reframing and changing a negative feeling into a positive one.

Step 1: Identify a situation for which a feeling exists that you would like to change. The feeling may be pain, hurt, anger, fear, envy, and so on.

Step 2: What is the payoff or advantage to feeling negatively? Do you gain power, control, prestige, a feeling of "poor me" or suffering? Answer the following question: How do I benefit from feeling _____?

Step 3: Could you feel differently? Is there another way to feel in this situation? A person who has angry feelings, for example, may also be seen as one who really cares about someone or something or one who wants to be involved with someone else. Someone who experiences fear may also be seen as a person who has the courage to show his or her feelings.

Step 4: Picture yourself feeling differently in this situation.

An example of the exercise: "A situation in which I felt bad involved my partner putting me down. I spent several minutes dressing and trying to look my best, and when I asked Ben how I looked, he just said 'okay.' I felt hurt, mad, and put down. The payoff was probably to get him to change his mind. I could feel differently by appreciating his honesty and feel good about knowing that he will always tell me what he thinks is the truth. I can picture myself feeling competent and secure in my relationship with Ben."

Loving Feeling #3:
Dealing with Anger and Joy

Most couples find it difficult to deal with emotions, especially extreme ones like anger and joy. In a marriage, you will experience anger and joy more frequently than in any other relationship. They should be regarded as normal, necessary emotions that are capable of teaching us something about ourselves. Joy and happiness teach us that we like what is going on. The bigger question is: What is our anger trying to tell us?

Anger is often triggered by fear, frustration, low self-esteem, and hurt feelings. You have a great deal at stake in your marriage. You and your spouse mean so much to each other; therefore, you both have the potential to hurt each other deeply. In marriage, people interact in more facets of their lives than in any other relationship. In short, marriage partners have the opportunity and the potential to evoke feelings of frustration, fear, and low self-esteem in each other, and these feelings may result in anger. To allow anger to be a constructive force in a relationship, you need to acknowledge that anger is an inevitable part of your life with your partner and learn how to deal with it when it occurs.

When you experience anger, you can either *vent* your feelings, *suppress* them, or *process* them with your partner. The following seven-step process is an effective way to deal with anger.

Step 1. Cool down from the heavy anger. Take a "time-out" from each other and separate physically.

When both of you are calm, you can begin to process. You begin the process by relaxing yourself through deep breathing and muscular relaxation procedures.

Step 2. Define the anger together, but agree that you won't attack, blame, or provoke each other. Ask yourself the following questions before you begin; they will help you to define the true reason for your anger.

What happened?
Who am I angry at?
What angers me most?

Step 3. Communicate with each other by using "I" messages and tentative guesses. Don't use accusing language; it will be counterproductive.

I feel angry with you when _____ because _____.
I feel most angry about _____ because _____.
The thing about this that angers me most is _____.

Consider what facet of your personality may trigger anger in this situation. Consider *reframing* (see Loving Feeling #2, page 46).

Step 4. After your discussion, each of you should prepare a separate statement in which you put the *other's* point of view in words. Each partner speaks for the other in a statement that clearly expresses how his or her partner sees the situation. You will know how your partner sees the situation because of the discussion you had in step 3.

Step 5. Exchange and correct, if necessary, what your

partner has written about your point of view. After you have done that, exchange the statements again (you know what you originally wrote). Each partner is free to change or modify the other's statements. This step can be done orally.

Step 6. Evaluate each other's position and list all available options and courses of action to take. Each partner should feel free to suggest whatever he or she believes is an alternative.

Step 7. With your partner, choose the option on which you both agree.

Remember, even though only one partner is angry, both of you have a responsibility to work through the anger together, thereby acknowledging that "you got angry with each other and together you need to find out exactly why." By exploring your thoughts and feelings together, as a couple, you may identify the primary emotion (e.g., fear, frustration, low self-esteem, or hurt feelings) that produced the anger in the first place. Now that you know what feelings caused your conflict, you can begin to solve it.

Identify one situation today in which you experienced anger with your partner and one situation in which you experienced joy. Use the seven-step process for angry feelings with your partner, if possible, or go through the process yourself and share your answers with your partner when he or she is available.

An example of a positive outcome from the exercise: "I usually feel angry when Becky says no to me sexually. I get quiet and pout in order to give her the 'silent treatment.' I hope this will hurt her for the injustice I feel and hopefully she will change her mind. I wish we both would try hard to do what the other person requests. When it isn't possible, we should identify a time when it will be."

Loving Feeling #4: Expressing Your Feelings

To be congruent is to express what you feel and experience at the moment. When couples express thoughts and feelings openly and honestly, true intimacy grows and grievances are revealed and resolved.

If you feel hurt or angry, you should trust your partner enough to honestly reveal to him or her what you are feeling without fearing that he or she will attack your feelings. In a marriage, congruent communication allows each partner to know what the other is feeling without guessing. When Diane feels angry at Stan for being late, she tells him. When Jim comes home and his wife has gone out without leaving a message indicating where she is, he expresses his feelings when she returns. This is called congruent communication. It gives each partner an opportunity to be empathetic and, as we have been showing you, no marriage can survive unless both partners empathize.

Granted, it takes courage to express feelings, but if you care enough about your relationship, each of you will be courageous enough to share perceptions and feelings. No issues should be off-limits. You should feel free to talk about your differences and feelings of anger, rejection, or despair.

One technique to use in learning to express your feelings is to state them in "I" messages. An "I" message has
three parts:

1. Describe the *behavior* without blaming.
2. State your *feelings*.
3. State what the *consequences* may be.

An example of an "I" message is "When you are *late*
coming home at night, I feel *anxious* because I think you
may have been in an *accident.*" In this example, "when
you are late coming home at night" describes the behavior, "I feel anxious" states your feeling, and "because I
think you may have been in an accident" states the consequences you fear.

State "I" messages for three different situations you
face today. Don't say things like "It's your fault" or
"You make me." Change these blaming statements into
the "I" message format. By accepting responsibility for
feelings, both partners can work together to change a
relationship from one of complaining to one of open,
honest communication.

Develop "I" messages that openly express the following emotions: fear, disappointment, pleasure, sadness,
hurt, resentment, anxiety, frustration, anger, joy, and
love.

Loving Feeling #5: Sharing Feelings

There are many verbal and nonverbal ways to express emotions and feelings. A smile, a frown, a clenched fist, an abrupt departure, and a slow walk are ways to express feelings without words. Happy, sad, furious, mad, titillated, and thrilled are words that convey feelings. Think of the ways that you express emotions to your partner without using words. Would you like to try a different way, perhaps one that you have been thinking about but have been unable to use? Try communicating in silence. Sit facing each other, touch hands, look into each other's eyes, and communicate love.

This exercise may not be as easy as it sounds. You may find that you are out of touch with your feelings altogether or you may find that you are able to experience some feelings but not others. You may be in touch with your feelings, but unable to express them. Or you may be in touch with some feelings and able to express them but not in touch with others. For example, Jim expresses anger well, but not fear. Sally expresses fear, but has a difficult time expressing joy. Don't be alarmed if this happens to you. Remember, recognizing the problem is the first step toward solving it.

If you find that you allow yourself to experience or express only those emotions you think are positive, like joy or pleasure, while you deny or bottle up those feelings that you think are negative, like anger or disappointment, you will likely seem distant, even lonely, when you and your partner are together. When you share your feelings, however, you will feel alive, real, and closer to each other.

The following exercise is designed to help you get in touch with sharing feelings and experiencing a higher level of emotional closeness, so that you can affirm and strengthen what works in your relationship.

Sit quietly and recall a time when you felt that you expressed yourself clearly to your partner. Remember what took place at the time when you felt most courageous. As you get in touch with that total experience, choose a time today when you can again use that courage and share a feeling in *words* with your partner. Share another in *writing,* maybe through a note, a letter, or a drawing, and yet another through *touch.*

As an extra activity, share with your partner how you would feel if you had more courage. Verbally tell your partner exactly what you would do (e.g., change careers or tell your mother-in-law to back off). What would *you* do?

Loving Feeling #6: Recapturing Feelings

Early in your relationship with your partner, you experienced certain strong emotions: "I can't keep my eyes off her," "I can only think of her," and "I have so many things that I want to share with him" are samples of powerful feelings. Many people feel that the strongest emotions are felt during the courtship period. Take a moment and re-create these old feelings now.

- Find a comfortable place, sit or lie down, close your eyes, and begin to concentrate on your breathing.
- Take *ten* long, slow breaths. Count to four for each inhale and exhale.
- Recall the first encounter with your partner. Remember the day and what it was like; remember what you were doing; remember how you felt.
- Reflect on these feelings and imagine re-creating the same feelings at some special time today.
- Open your eyes. You should feel refreshed.
- Pick a time to re-create these feelings today.

Loving Feeling #7: Creating Feelings

Fantasize about a relationship that you would consider ideal. What is it about this relationship that you would like in your marriage? Think the same feelings and visualize the same images as you look at your partner. Act out this new feeling and share it with your partner.

Share this or another romantic fantasy with your partner on one occasion today. After you share the fantasy, discuss with your partner how you can make part of your fantasy happen. If you can't do all of it today, make plans to do it soon. Keep these feelings alive.

Identify a positive part of your partner's body. Tell him or her how you feel about it and explain your feelings.

Take one time segment (i.e., dinner, evening hours) and decide to feel differently with your partner.

Loving Feeling #8: Sentence Stems

Complete the following sentence stems to stimulate feelings of love. Each person should answer separately and exchange sentences with his or her partner.

I can remember feeling love when _____
Sometimes today I feel love when _____
Sometimes when I feel love I _____
Sometimes I try to hide my love by _____
One of the disguised ways my love comes out is _____
If I were more accepting of my feelings of love _____
If I were willing to express my love fully _____
Sometimes when I was younger the frightening thing about fully expressing my love was _____
If I were willing to breathe deeply and feel my love fully _____
I can remember feeling loved when _____
Sometimes I try to deny feeling loved by _____
If I were more accepting when I feel loved _____
If I were willing to let others see that I feel loved _____
Sometimes the frightening thing about admitting I feel loved is _____
I am becoming aware _____
I am beginning to suspect _____
If people knew how much love I have locked up inside me _____

·4·

Time for Loving Behavior

C reating a meaningful marriage requires each partner to make time to behave in ways that express his or her love for the other. There are *countless opportunities* for spouses to share loving behaviors. They can listen, understand, call, be companions, or engage in helping or playing with each other. They can send flowers or gifts, touch or hold, or be patient and caring. The possibilities for being loving are endless.

As you start to behave in a loving way, you will feel better as your actions express your feelings. There will be less of a feeling of obligation (I should) and more of a feeling of satisfaction (I am). Behavior conveys the real message between partners. What a person says matters less; behavior is what counts. You can tell your partner, "I'd like to spend more time walking and talking," but if you never do it or make time for it, you are saying, in effect, that your message is not important. The same principle applies in a marital relationship. You can talk endlessly about the things you would like to do, but in practice what you actually do communicates what you have decided to do.

Despite what you say, the relationship you have is the relationship you want. Your present relationship is a reflection of what you are actually putting into it. If you experience fighting and bickering in your relationship, the chances are you are doing something to create the situations that elicit that type of behavior. You usually know what will provoke a fight with your spouse. Behaviors like insisting on getting your own way or failing to respect your partner usually guarantee lack of cooperation. Any behavior, good or bad, that continues to exist within a relationship is being reinforced. If your partner continues to challenge you or insist he or she is right, you must stop and ask yourself, "How am I helping this behavior to continue? When I fight, yell, or give in, is it possible that is what my partner is seeking?" The behavior you notice and reward is behavior that will continue. To have a loving relationship, you must reinforce loving behaviors and ignore harmful ones, so that they are not reinforced. The suggestions we include are brief, but are designed to produce positive results in your relationship.

Loving Behavior #1: Encouraging Days

Any day can become more energizing and encouraging when you develop a positive, courageous outlook because only then will the countless opportunities to encourage your spouse become readily apparent. Consider the following: Jerry got up on time and noticed Nancy was still asleep and the children were not getting ready for school. He had reminded her that he'd need breakfast early, and there was a shirt to iron for his appointment. He was disappointed and angry. Before waking her, he caught himself and chose a different feeling. He said, "Good morning, Honey. It's a bit late and I have that trip to make. I'll get the kids ready for school and start the breakfast. Remember it's the blue shirt I need." This significant change in his behavior turned a potentially hostile start for the day into a cooperative beginning. It did not take more time or energy to change his approach, but the outcome was positive and everyone was able to enjoy his or her day. Any day, whether encouraging or discouraging, is based on your ability to spot the potential for positive relationships and to make them happier.

"Encouraging days" is an activity that focuses on identifying behaviors that will both please you and stimulate encouraging behaviors in your spouse. It is important to be able to identify the specific behaviors that please you and to be able to respond to the behaviors that your spouse has indicated pleases him or her. When you fail to identify the behaviors you would appreciate, you are discounting your value and your needs. If you fail to encourage your partner, you are not willing to encourage and build his or her feelings of worth. By identifying and asking for behaviors that will please you, you communicate that you feel good about yourself and are able to appreciate yourself. Valuing ourselves enables us to value others. Encouraging days build not only the self-esteem of each partner but also provide for the ability to cooperate.

For the following activity, you should list ten small,

pleasant behaviors that your partner can do to please you. These behaviors should be specific, positive, and unrelated to past conflicts. Choose behaviors that are possible for your partner to do on a daily basis, for example, "Call me and tell me you love me," "Take a ten-minute walk with me," "Give me a hug," "Share something you're feeling or thinking," "Help with the laundry," "Do the grocery shopping," and "Watch the children while I go out."

Exchange lists with your partner. Each partner should then choose to do at least two encouraging behaviors each day. When your partner does something for you that was on your list, show your appreciation by saying, "I liked the way you thought of me," "I appreciate that you did that," or "It was thoughtful of you to . . ." At the end of each week, meet and update the lists, adding at least two more behaviors that would be encouraging.

You'll be amazed at how quickly this activity works to provide concrete encouragement. You will notice a definite increase in positive behaviors between you and your partner if you place no demand on your partner to respond to anything on the list, and if you put nothing on the list that has been an issue or reason for conflict in the past. For example, if you disagree about going to plays or athletic events, do not put it on the list. The list is not for issues and challenges. The activity should open the door for more encouraging, cooperative behavior. The emphasis here is on becoming aware of the behaviors that encourage positive actions. It also helps you to tune into the needs of your partner. Thus it also opens the door to your being more aware of your own needs, disclosing or sharing them, with the goal of developing a mutually respectful and satisfying relationship.

Because encouragement is a powerful tool in improving relationships, we suggest that you and your partner use it regularly as a way of providing time for each other in a loving relationship.

Loving Behavior #2: One-Minute Hugs

Jeanie was hurt and angry that Ed never seemed to have time for closeness anymore. Sexual contact was seldom and routine. They never sat near each other and carefully avoided touching as they moved about the house. Jeanie had been taught that the man was supposed to originate contact, but she could no longer stand the growing distance between them. One evening before supper as Ed was passing her, she stepped in front of him and gave him a big, long hug. He was surprised, but said he enjoyed it. The hug broke down the wall between them. If you want contact, don't wait, initiate.

Touch is perhaps the most powerful and meaningful way of expressing love, appreciation, and concern. Often couples will complain that they don't have time to show affection because of their busy lives and the many responsibilities they have that keep them apart.

The one-minute hug is designed to eliminate the excuse that there isn't enough time. The one-minute hug can be done spontaneously but obviously requires the cooperation of both partners. It is best when it is spontaneous and it communicates the genuine, positive feel-

ings each partner feels for the other. The one-minute hug
then becomes a bond in the marriage. It is a recommit-
ment and a restatement of the strong feelings between
the partners. The one-minute hug is a positive, effective
way to communicate feelings that are present but that
cannot be expressed in a short period of time. In one
minute, the hug can communicate much more than a
minute's worth of words. Your hug should express genuine feelings and should be comfortable, not forced. You
may decide to end the hug with a kiss. Even though it is
"infectious," spreading love is desirable.

Loving Behavior #3: Encouragement Meetings

Betty and Sam were both well educated and perceptive.
They had a talent for identifying mistakes in each other
and pointing them out. Of course, each claimed he or she
was only doing this to help the other become a better
person, in order to be more proud of his or her "almost
perfect" partner. They had become superb faultfinders
and nitpickers, able to identify ties that were not straight,
slips showing under skirts, incorrect grammar, and more
on their lengthy lists of faults. They were beginning to
drive each other crazy.

Fortunately for them, Betty and Sam have tremendous
potential for becoming encouragers. Because they are
able to identify all kinds of small defects, they need only
switch to a positive perspective and comment only on
things they appreciate.

This switch to encouragement is the foundation of all loving relationships. Encouragement focuses on the positive aspects of the relationship, identifying anything that is positive or has the potential for good in the relationship. Encouragement is concerned with reaffirming the partner's value while building self-esteem. Encouragement showers the partner with the positive observations that often go unexpressed.

An encouraging marital relationship is one in which there is effective listening, respect, and enthusiasm, as each partner focuses on the other's strengths, assets, and resources. That person's efforts and contributions are thus recognized, and there is the all-important feeling of empathy between the partners. In an encouraging relationship, one can *always* see something positive in one's partner. Encouraging behavior precedes the willingness to engage in "encouragement meetings." When each spouse has increased his or her positive relationship behaviors, encouragement meetings are even more appropriate.

The encouragement meeting provides a more regular, systematic way to strengthen the marriage. Its purpose is to allow partners to share the positive things they see in each other and in their relationship. We have found that encouragement meetings can be held both spontaneously and on a scheduled basis. How you plan to do it is up to you. The five guidelines that follow are basic to the encouragement meeting:

1. Meet in a place and at a time that is quiet and free from interruption.

2. Sit facing each other, close enough to hold hands comfortably.

3. One partner begins by saying, "Something I appreciate about you today is . . ." Then the partner continues by saying, "I like, appreciate, or enjoy . . ." The partner who speaks first takes no more than two minutes. The listening partner maintains eye contact, indicates attentiveness, and does not interrupt.

The partner may say, "Something I appreciate about you today is your willingness to cooperate, even when I know you would rather not. I appreciate your going to the game and keeping me company. It makes me want to cooperate with your interests, too."

4. At the end of two minutes the listening partner briefly feeds back the ideas, beliefs, feelings, or values heard, taking care not to challenge them. This means the listening partner has indicated what was heard without any challenge. Being heard is also encouraging.

5. Then the process is repeated, using the same sentences. The other partner begins, "Something I appreciate about you today is . . ."

When the couple is comfortable with this simple encouragement meeting format, additional topics may be used, for example: "The most enjoyable thing I did today was . . . ," "Something I value about you is . . . ," "The most positive thing in our relationship is . . . ," or "I like or enjoy . . ." The encouragement meeting adds considerable energy, enthusiasm, love, and caring to the marriage because it focuses on what is positive and it regularly recognizes even the simple things that are going well.

Loving Behavior #4: One-Minute Appreciation

Fred has just returned from a training session focusing on positive thinking in the workplace. He was amused at how well he could apply the concepts at work and how poorly he applied them at home. He decided it was time to change the home atmosphere he had created.

He found Sue and said, "We've got to talk." She anticipated a list of complaints and was not enthusiastic; however, as he began to share what he appreciated about her and their relationship, she was totally surprised. Fred said, "I feel I'm not letting you know how much I appreciate your attention to the children. I am very proud of the time you have invested in them. I also know you go to special efforts to find and prepare foods that are on the diet I have selected. I feel you are always thinking of the family. I want you to know how pleased I am with you." Fred and Sue decided they should do this both spontaneously and regularly.

This talk can be conducted like a typical TV advertisement. You have only one minute and you need to communicate all the things you appreciate in that time. It will usually require preparation to use the time most effectively. Comment continuously for a full minute on things you appreciate, like, enjoy, respect, or value in your partner. *Do not do it with any qualifier* (e.g., sort of, kind of); *make it a full appreciation.* This is a valuable exercise because it is done without any reservations. It allows you to completely value your partner.

Loving Behavior #5:
The "I Love You" Note

Jim and Stacey were often leaving each other reminders and "to do" notes that covered the full range of their busy daily lives. Although they were busy, they were never too busy to forget about leaving the notes regarding grocery shopping, the dog, bills, appointments, and so on. They could always find time to communicate what they wanted their partner to do, but they did not have time to share the positive.

One day Stacey returned to see notes posted everywhere. It was exhausting for her to contemplate what was expected. In her fatigue she wondered why she and Jim communicated only directions and never their feelings. "Aren't we worth more to each other than all of this trivia and business? Is our marriage and relationship expressed only by a series of directions and 'to do's'?"

Stacey then composed an "I love you" note to Jim and removed all of her other notes. When Jim returned, he was thrilled with the idea. They found a different way to communicate important reminders and issues.

The "I love you" note to your partner develops a brief and effective way to express your positive, loving thoughts. Much like the Browning poem, "How do I love thee, let me count the ways . . . ," it gives you a process for counting the ways you love your partner. In the love note you can talk about things you want to do for your partner, positive attitudes, patience, cooperation, caring, or any other traits that are present but are usually not recognized. You can deliver these notes to your partner in a variety of ways. You could use the mail; put them in the pockets of dresses or suits; or in a brief-case; or inside a wallet or purse; place them inside a special dresser drawer; stick them on the refrigerator; place them under a dinner plate; or hide them inside the person's automobile. Find as many creative ways of delivering "I love you" notes as possible. This behavior encourages you to put in writing the positive feelings you have for your partner and to openly share these feelings at any time and in many ways.

Loving Behavior #6: Choosing Positive Actions

When something happens, we have a choice about how we respond. Sometimes this option is overlooked in the flurry of activity.

Janice had received a promotion at work and was now under increased pressure to produce. There were more and more demands at work, and the children had their own schoolwork and obligations, which took up most of her free time. Her husband, Mike, was the one person she could say no to, and it was apparent that she was doing this regularly. When Janice reevaluated her priorities and the important relationships in her life, it was apparent that she should be more considerate of Mike. They set aside some time to discuss in a positive way how they could consider all the demands on Janice and still cooperate with each other.

Choosing positive actions suggests that you take the time to consider the typical communication that occurs when your partner requests something instead of making a hasty negative reply. At times, one or both members of any partnership will develop a negative reaction pattern. In other words, no matter what is suggested, you or your partner will tend to respond in a negative instead of a positive way.

For example, the negative reactor chooses to react negatively to anything that is suggested. Thus, they oppose both getting up earlier and going to bed later, whichever is suggested. They are "aginners." They know what they are against, which at times seems like everything, and they take pleasure in being powerful by refusing to cooperate. Their place in life and their power come from being in opposition.

In this instance, the challenge is to change the habitual negative-response mechanism and replace it with a positive action within the relationship. But you must first recognize the reason why this negative behavior occurs. Sometimes being negative gets you attention or power; at other times you use it to get even with your partner. If you take on an active, positive-response point of view, you will immediately have more enthusiasm toward your partner, and the positive energy this generates can bring about constructive changes. The next time you are in a situation where you are inclined to say no, stop for a moment and find a reason to say yes or to be more cooperative.

Recall a situation in which you responded in a negative

• While exhaling, let your entire body go limp. Experience a wave of heaviness and warmth in your body.

• Resume normal daily activity. If you feel rushed, overwhelmed, and have lost your sense of humor and perspective on life, consider seeing a funny movie, listening to music, or taking a walk. Anything that makes you say, "I value myself and I am giving myself this time" qualifies as a valuing activity.

Even this brief amount of time alone can restore your internal balance. You can also help yourself develop a new perspective on your relationship. After you learn to value yourself, you will be in a better position to value your partner.

Loving Behavior #9:
Fun, Play, and Enjoyment

Fun and play are basic to a sense of satisfaction and enthusiasm about a relationship. They help you look forward with positive anticipation to being together.

How much zest and fun exist in your relationship? Do you still find each other stimulating? Do you look forward to being together because you know it will spark something positive in both of you?

Being able to put stressful events into perspective while maintaining a sense of humor is another essential element in a marriage. Even newly married couples experience situations that were considered serious at the time but can later be looked back on as humorous. Try to remember one or two of those events from your own marriage. Label them with a brief term or even a single word that can be shared with your spouse to recall the situation. Those few words can be used to turn around stressful events and bring the incident into perspective. One couple who had broken a lounge chair while attempting to make love on it use the key word *lounge* to signal to each other the importance of seeing things in perspective. Do you remember events in your relationship that would be useful to help you and your spouse see things in perspective?

If the feeling of fun has gone out of your relationship, there are a number of things you can do. First, think about the activities you can do together that you both enjoy, (e.g., watching or playing sports or going to a concert, a play, or a movie). Then make plans to do these things together regularly to renew the feeling of mutual pleasure and enjoyment.

Very often what attracted you most to your partner—companionship, fun, the opportunity to share time in an enjoyable way—is lost as your marriage progresses. We suggest that you develop a list of activities that you both enjoy, which will become your "fun" list. Keep it available and consult it on a regular basis. Your fun list may include walking, going to a play, singing, swimming, taking a walk. If you enjoy doing things that your partner does not, develop an agreement between the two of you that encourages each partner to pursue separately the things he or she takes pleasure in. You don't have to be dependent on your spouse for all of your fun activities.

Loving Behavior #10: Plan a Mystery Event for Your Partner Each Month

One of the ways of caring is to identify the activities your partner enjoys and to plan mystery outings to those places and events, (e.g., athletic events, civic events, theater, concerts, zoo, museums). You make the arrangements and get the tickets.

Loving Behavior #11: Switch Your Typical Roles

If you always plan or initiate activities, encourage your partner to begin initiating plans. A marriage, as we've learned, is a partnership, and each partner is responsible for holding up his or her end. If one partner makes all the plans, he or she is really keeping the other person from functioning and expressing him- or herself fully in the marriage. Consider your relationship: Who usually initiates the hugging, kissing, sex, getting tickets for an event, sharing positive feelings? Change places occasionally and let the other person become the initiator.

Loving Behavior #12: Increasing Dating Activities

Step 1: Sit down with your partner and write out separately a list of activities you would like to do together. Do not include activities you know your partner does not enjoy. These activities should include a range of choices, from quick to time-consuming, cheap to expensive. Here's a sample list:

- Re-create activities you enjoyed when you were dating.
- Go out to dinner.
- Read a book together.
- Have dinner at home by fire or candlelight.
- Watch a good movie on TV or videocassette.
- Go for a picnic.
- Go to a football game.
- Spend a weekend in a motel or camping.
- Give and get a massage and a hug.
- Take pictures.
- Garden.
- Learn a new sport.
- Cook a meal together.
- Go to the theater.
- Spend time together and discuss the day's activities.
- Play a sport, i.e., racquetball, tennis, golf.
- Take a walk.

Keep your list of activities current and add to it as your interests develop.

Step 2: After both of you have written out your lists, read through each other's list and try to decide on the activities that you want to do together. The following three rules will help you narrow your activity choices:

1. Be prepared to try new activities. You may be surprised by how much you enjoy them.

2. Be flexible in combining activities. You may be able to include activities you enjoy alone but would like to share with your partner.

3. Do not do something you do not like. The idea of this exercise is to enjoy yourself. There is no point in one partner unwillingly doing something that he or she definitely will not enjoy. This will only cause problems.

Step 3: Arrange a specific time for the planned date.

Step 4: Choose a time each month or week to make specific plans for your dates as a couple.

Extension: Make some plans for the future. Sit down together and talk over some long-range plans. Just talking about future plans, whether they happen or not, can help you both feel more committed to the relationship. Overall, the good things of the past, as well as expected good events, are all-important in adding to the feeling of enjoyment and sense of commitment that you and your partner have for your relationship.

·5·

Developing a Sound Marital System

Y our marriage is your most important relationship. You may not get what you want from it, however, because you don't understand the factors that influence the marital system. This system is a reflection of the goals, beliefs, priorities, and values people share as a couple. When you and your partner's goals are in alignment, or when you are cooperating, the marriage system usually functions smoothly. You may each have career objectives and recreational objectives that are unique, but they can be reached without creating friction. When goals are aligned so that there is cooperation, each partner has room to reach his or her goals with the support of the other.

Jim and Laura are both interested in health and physical conditioning. Jim likes to play tennis for several hours three times a week. Laura goes to an aerobics class three times a week. They schedule their time so that they can watch the children while their partner is exercising. It also means that the couple has common goals that are as important as their personal goals. Their common goal is to have the whole family participate in a local church and to conduct family meetings to keep communication channels open. They are free to pursue their goals while they continue to work toward the goals of the marriage.

When you develop a system of relating with your partner that is open and understanding, you have more ways to relate in a positive manner. Without an open system that promotes understanding, conflict can develop. If you place a high priority on watching football, being involved in clubs or civic affairs, or playing tennis or golf, this external commitment affects your marital relationship adversely.

We have a simple formula that illustrates the basis of a sound marital system. $MH = SE + SI + SH$. To translate: Marital Happiness is based on Self-Esteem (that is, the self-esteem of each partner, which comes from his or her own internal feelings of worth and is not dependent on the evaluation of the partner or anyone else), plus Social Interest (willingness to cooperate in the give-and-take of the relationship), plus a Sense of Humor (the ability to see him- or herself and the relationship in perspective). When a couple is not overwhelmed by any of the tension and friction in their relationship, but is able to see that there is a positive and humorous potential to everything that happens, their marriage will be a happy one.

Carl wonders about the system he and Jean have for conflict resolution. When things are not going Jean's way, she withdraws and refuses to communicate. Carl, on the other hand, has learned that if he yells and screams, Jean will usually concede. He recognizes their methods are similar to those of their children, ages five and seven.

Jennifer often wonders about the type of communication she and Frank have in their marriage. Some of her friends say their husbands never talk. That is not Jennifer's problem. Frank and Jennifer talk all the time, but it is a combative type of interaction. They make demands on each other and question each other's motives. They each know what they want and what they want from the relationship, but they haven't made the effort to determine what their partner wants. If they become aware of their partner's needs, they identify how they fit with their needs. If they don't fit, they will be challenged.

This system does not work because it produces a lot of stress and tension. There is a better way of communicating—through the daily dialogue.

Loving System #1: Regular Dialogue

Much has been written about the importance of communication in a marital relationship, and communication is indeed one of the most important skills for a successful marriage. Unfortunately, little has been written about *how to* communicate. It is apparent to us from our observations and studies of couples who have effective relationships that they do things differently than the couples we see who have problems communicating. We know that one of the most effective activities for the development of marital happiness and an effective communication system is the regular dialogue. If you find that doing the dialogue everyday is too demanding, we suggest that you do it as regularly as you can handle it. Any change in a relationship takes time to get used to, so start slowly if you have to, but remember, we all have within ourselves the capacity to accomplish a great deal more than we think we can. So try to do this dialogue on a daily basis; it will be to your advantage.

To do the dialogue, set aside ten minutes a day. Allow five minutes for each of you to express your feelings. When one person talks, the other listens and no comments are permitted. When you share your feelings, share your real self and what you're experiencing at the moment, including your emotions, beliefs, goals, and values. As you do this, you will gain a deeper understanding, greater self-awareness, and fuller acceptance of yourself and your partner. If you do this daily dialogue, your relationship will become less of a mystery and more of a joy. What had been assumed will now become more clearly understood by each partner. The daily dialogue helps you to learn to accept what your partner is saying and to share your feelings with greater ease. You may feel uncomfortable at first, but as you proceed, the benefits of open communication will encourage you to participate more openly.

Couples often ask us, "What is it that we are going to be sharing?" The answer is simple: You share what is on your mind, what is in your heart, and what you're experiencing (e.g., your hopes and fears, the things you're excited about, the things you're anxious about, your joys and sorrows, your pride and embarrassment, the things you are fearful or apprehensive about, your feelings of inadequacy, your feelings of anger, your feelings of enthusiasm). This dialogue allows couples to share the important things that rarely are shared but are essential information for people who have come to love each other. It is important to recognize that the dialogue is not an opportunity for you to ventilate or attempt to manipulate by making your partner responsible for your emotions. It is not a time to make demands or requests.

As you grow in self-awareness, you will come to feel more in charge of your life, and as you become more aware of yourself and your partner's needs and feelings, you will know how to comfort, encourage, and help. Dialogue works as potential to bring new enthusiasm, energy, and vitality into the marital relationship.

Activity: Schedule a number of dialogue sessions for the coming week. Pick a specific time and place. You may begin with daily dialogue, or perhaps dialogue three times a week. As you progress, you will find the dialogue more valuable. The number of times you dialogue per week and the amount of time you reserve for the dialogue are up to you. The evidence indicates that dialoguing needs to be held on a regular basis to be effective.

Loving System #2: Resolving Conflict

If you think that continuous conflict is a normal and essential component of a marriage relationship, you may have observed a model of conflict in your own family when you were growing up. You may also have seen a number of television shows that depict marriage as a battleground. This is not the way it should be. Happily married people should live in relative harmony. Although differences will occur, your marriage should not be a constant battle in either active or passive terms.

When Tom and Linda have a difference of opinion or are in conflict, they try to get it out in the open; however, in a short period of time, one or the other, at times both, has hurt feelings and withdraws. This is followed by a period of smoldering feelings. Although each clearly adopts a posture of "things are OK, I'm not discussing it," the subtle hostility obviously clogs the gears of cooperation. Silence is a devastating way to handle conflicts. When there is silence, you start to assume what your partner is thinking and this may increase hostility. You also start to feel more upset because there is a power struggle between you.

Al and Shirley came from homes where both father and mother said everything that was on their minds. There were no restraints. The conflict was resolved when one partner was emotionally destroyed. This was the couple's only model. When they have conflicts, each battles to get his or her way, and there is no give-and-take. Conflict always results in anger and hurt feelings unless you have a system for handling conflict.

The reality of marriage is that there are a number of challenges to "living happily ever after." Put together in a relationship two persons who come from varied backgrounds and there is always potential for conflict. Most of us have learned to express our negative feelings openly and intensively. We also have high expectations that others should meet our needs. So it is not surprising that couples, after a period of time, find it difficult to reach agreement on even the most simple issues. Worse than that, they often may not know what the real issues are. We have developed a simple process for resolving conflict that will help you identify an effective method for conflict resolution.

Step 1: Show mutual respect. Very often in a conflict situation the issue or the topic being talked about is not as important as the attitude of the partners in regard to the conflict. Unless the relationship is based on mutual respect, it is very difficult to develop the intent to end the conflict. Mutual respect involves understanding your partner's feelings and beliefs and indicating that he or she is heard and understood. Mutual respect also involves dealing with each other as equals. As mutual respect develops, each partner seeks to understand and respect the other's point of view. Respect is the most important factor in a loving relationship.

Step 2: Pinpoint the real issue. When embroiled in a conflict situation, most couples have difficulty identifying the real issue. The issue on the surface tends to appear superficial: Who does what chore around the house, how much money is spent, or what type of sexual relationship is desired. These are all genuine disagreements, but the real issues are buried and can be found only when one partner begins to understand the goals and priorities of the other. The real issue often centers around one of the following:

• You feel your status or prestige is being threatened. "Why should I give in?" "What will people think if I let my partner do this?" "Why doesn't my partner understand how this affects my standing with other people?"

• You feel your superiority is being challenged. "If I'm not in charge, I feel inadequate." "I have to win and when I don't I feel very uncomfortable and angry."

• Unless you're in control, you feel your right to decide is at stake. "If I don't win and show my partner how to do things, he or she won't do it right." "Why should I let my partner decide for me when it's up to me to be in control or in charge?"

• You feel your judgment is not being considered; you're being treated unfairly. "Since my way is the best way, why are we arguing about this?"

• You feel hurt and need to retaliate or get even. "After all, my partner won the last battle and it's my turn," or "I'm going to get even this time."

When you have finally pinpointed the issue by being in touch with the feelings of your spouse, such as identifying who controls or resents control, you will be able to discuss alternative ways to behave and reach a new agreement that is satisfactory to each of you. You have to be aware of your goals and priorities and be willing to cooperate and compromise. Only you can change your priorities.

Step 3: Seek areas of agreement. In a conflict situation a more comfortable solution is usually to ask your mate how he or she would alleviate the problem. However, it is more effective for each of you to ask, "What can *I* do to change the difficulties in this relationship?" The only person you have the potential to be in total control of is yourself. When you and your partner decide what you are willing to do, you create an atmosphere in which agreement can be reached quickly. Work to identify what you agree on. For example, both of you may believe you are right, that you feel hurt, that you want the pain to stop. Although the ultimate solution to conflict involves change for both of you, you quickly open the door for resolution of conflict when you show you desire it and recognize that the decision to change is the responsibility of each person. As couples learn to cooperate rather than fight for their rights, they discover what they can do to resolve a conflict.

Step 4: Participate mutually in decisions. Only after you work together on problems to identify the issue and find areas of agreement can you develop a tentative solution. After you have agreed to this point, each of you may then respond by either accepting the solution as is or by modifying it. This should be done in an atmosphere of give-and-take. For example, "I would be willing to go out to dinner twice a month if you would agree to go to medium-price restaurants that are within our budget," or "I would be willing to go dancing twice a month if you'd agree to leave by midnight," or "I would agree to join the bowling league if you'd also be willing to participate with me in some mixed-doubles tennis."

When your agreement is reached and it is clear what each partner's role is in carrying out the decision, progress has been made toward conflict resolution.

Ground rules for resolving conflicts: It is also important to recognize a few simple fundamentals. Set a limit on the amount of time that you will spend discussing problems. Marriage is not designed to be a continuous round of debate and arguing; a much larger amount of time for enjoyment is needed. When your partner has developed habits that are difficult or destructive for your relationship, it is important to allow some time for him or her to change.

Apply the four-step conflict resolution (on pages 83–85) when you are both interested in cooperating and are committed to resolving a conflict. To make the exercise more effective, each of you should do the following:

• Show mutual respect. Be willing to listen and to understand the other person's point of view. Respect that point of view even if you disagree with it. Do not try to overpower your partner.

• Pinpoint the real issue. Identify for yourself what you feel is behind the reason you are in conflict. Are you feeling threatened? Is your feeling of being in control or being right being challenged? Do you feel hurt or do you want to get even? What are you feeling when you are in conflict? That feeling will direct you to the real issue, which is usually your goals and priorities.

• Seek areas of agreement. Instead of deciding that your partner should change, ask "What can I do to change the relationship?" Create a cooperative atmosphere. Usually each partner will find ways to compromise.

• Mutually participate in decisions. Develop solutions that are mutually agreeable and in which each person feels respected. The relationship can become a win-win relationship instead of a self-defeating contest.

This proven format for resolving conflict has helped many couples reach an agreement while still feeling loved and valued.

Loving System #3: Dealing with Impasses

One of the most disruptive factors in a marital system is the impasse. An impasse occurs when one or both partners feel they've reached a point at which they are unwilling to change or move and their partner appears to expect something of them that they are not willing to do. These impasses are part of what we call the *resistance process.* This resistance process occurs when one partner is committed to forcing a change while the other is equally committed to resisting that change. Impasses bring about considerable tension and discomfort in a relationship.

When Nancy and John have a difference of opinion, it often develops into an impasse. The impasse occurs when they feel they are unwilling to change or compromise. They both know they are right and can't understand how the other person can see the situation differently. Impasses tend not to be resolved when no progress is then possible because each person is unwilling to give in. If they can't agree on the type of new car they want, they keep the old one. If they disagree on which movie to see, they stay home. They have learned that neither will give in, and each partner has learned to become more stubborn and determined. Unless this behavior changes, their marriage will not be happy.

If you and your partner are often at an impasse, recognizing it and changing this pattern will provide you with an opportunity to create a new and more satisfying relationship by helping you to meet previously unmet needs. You become aware of untouched personal and emotional resources. By dealing with an impasse, you are capable of making a negative situation positive, thereby opening a pathway to a mutually fulfilling relationship.

Some impasses are resolved naturally when your love for each other is stronger than each partner's need to be right or to win. Others can be solved only if you and your partner learn to appreciate and accept the differences between you. You can value and appreciate your partner's different point of view only if you see it as his or her uniqueness. Remember, love does not depend on 100-percent agreement. Love is understanding, patient, and willing to compromise. When you have identified an impasse, the following activity will help you become familiar with the process of solving it.

1. Be patient, take your time. Do not try to force a solution. It takes patience and cooperation to initiate change when resistance has been established.

2. Listen closely to what your partner is communicating. Practice active listening by listening to the feelings expressed and communicating back to your partner exactly what you've heard about his or her goals, beliefs, priorities, feelings, or values to confirm that you understand exactly what is being said. Get the whole message.

3. Use "I" messages. State your feelings clearly, not in a hostile way but in a sharing manner. Begin by saying,

"I feel . . ." Identify your reason for the feeling. When you use an "I" message, you will communicate clearly.

4. Break the resistance by suggesting and considering alternatives to the impasse. The person who feels resistance should ask for time to consider alternatives. Consider together any possible alternatives to the impasse. Record all possible solutions and don't reject any until you have considered all of them. Begin by identifying what *you* would do differently to break the impasse. Don't expect your partner to give in. Recognize your relationship by changing yourself.

5. Specify areas of mutual agreements and areas of disagreements. Identify first the places where you appear to be in agreement. Each partner should list the areas in which he or she feels there is agreement (e.g., parenting, religion, recreational time). This step is important because it is encouraging to identify areas that you both feel positive about regarding a particular impasse. It gives you a foundation to work with. Next, clearly identify what each of you feels is the reason for the disagreement.

6. Confine the discussion to the central topic. Don't attack, be sarcastic, or be concerned with winning. In this situation each person must demonstrate his or her ability to cooperate and willingness to give-and-take in the relationship.

Guidelines for Discussing Impasses:

- Listen and acknowledge that you understand your partner's beliefs and feelings. At this point, acknowledgment does not mean you accept these beliefs and feelings but that you understand them.

Taking Time for Love

- Stay focused on the topic and each other's point of view.
- Share your thoughts and feelings openly with each other.
- Encourage your partner's willingness or efforts to change.
- Be patient. It took time to develop the impasse and it will take time to reduce the resistance.
- Be responsible for making changes in your own behavior to help resolve the impasse.

7. Take turns talking and listening. Do not get involved in conversations that attack or go in circles.

8. Reverse roles with your partner and state how you think he or she perceives the situation. In this role reversal, talk as if you were the other person. The other person should not interrupt you but wait until you've concluded your role reversal statement. Then your partner should tell you if what you said was accurate or not and why.

If the impasse remains unsolved, establish another time to discuss the problem. An impasse may remain unsolved because each person may be convinced he or she is right or is being treated unfairly. If you enter the activity without a desire to recognize your own erroneous perceptions and limitations, then you will not be willing to compromise. As you become aware of your perceptions and that you have a choice, you can resolve the impasse and develop greater happiness for you and your partner. Do the following to resolve an impasse:

- Be open to your partner's ideas.
- Look at the problem from your partner's perspective.
- Identify and brainstorm possible alternatives and solutions.
- Think about what you can do to solve the problem.
- Agree to take the steps that indicate a willingness on both sides to give in and cooperate.

Loving System #4: Respect

Because of their need to feel free, liberated, and independent, Lyn and George exert their rights but sometimes do it in a manner that creates friction. George says, "I've got a season pass for football, so don't count on me to be around on Saturdays." Lyn is distraught. She knows she will be responsible for the shopping and managing three young children all day. She feels she's not respected and wants to get even.

Respect is the essential element in a happy and productive marriage. Respect is even more important than communication or equality. Respect goes beyond the usual communication and understanding we experience. To respect your partner, you must be willing and able to:

- Listen to your partner's opinions and indicate through words and/or actions that you understand.
- Care about your mate's concerns.
- Value your partner's point of view.

- Be able to recognize, accept, and value not only the ways in which you are alike but also the ways in which you are different.

An activity that supports respect in a relationship involves granting each person the right to choose and go in the directions that are productive for him or her. Each partner has an equal right to choose productive directions as long as he or she does not harm the relationship. Meet with your partner to focus on increasing respect.

Another activity that works to confirm respect is to have a brief meeting with your spouse during which each of you completes the following sentences: "I respect you because _____," "I respect myself because _____," "When we respect each other _____." Make an effort to put respect into action in your relationship because no marriage can survive without it.

Choose from the following issues those in your relationship that lack respect. Discuss them with your mate using the guidelines for respect discussed above.

Sexuality.
Dependability.
Taking turns choosing recreational outings.
Sharing household tasks.
Socializing with friends.
Financial decisions.

Loving System #5: Choosing to Spend More Quality Time Together

Carl and Linda are at the point where they have no relationship with each other. They are so busy pursuing their own interests and raising the children that they have little time to spend alone together. They have tried to resolve the problem by setting aside some time each weekend to be alone. They would rent a movie and watch it together at home. Like many couples, they don't like the situation they are in, but they don't know where to begin or how to change the situation. The best place to begin is with yourself. If you are dissatisfied, share your feelings with your partner. If you agree, then meet and identify some quality activities you could initiate together.

Marital relationships move from the premarital phase, in which each partner seems to have a tremendous need to spend every available minute with his or her partner, to the recognition that little quality time is spent together. The couple start to take each other for granted and become bored with each other. When this happens, it is important to determine how much of the time you spend together can be considered "quality" time. In quality time a person has a high level of interest in and derives a great deal of enjoyment from the activity.

In your relationship the quality of your time together is more important than the quantity. Analyze your daily, weekly, and monthly schedules to determine the amount of time you and your partner actually spend together.

What percentage of the time is quality time? Look at next week's schedule: What plans are already made? Can you make arrangements to spend more quality time with your partner?

Here are some questions to ask yourself regarding use and scheduling of your time.

- Do I feel that I am in control of my time?
- Do we each try to avoid overscheduling?
- Does either of us watch television excessively?
- Do we take enough time to keep up with each other's joys, problems, or concerns?
- Do we make time to maintain effective contacts with valued friends and family members?
- Do we find time, separately and together, for creative leisure activities?
- Do we each have adequate amounts of private time alone for reflection or meditation?

If you realize that you and your partner need more time together, use the following guidelines to help you work out a schedule that will allow you to spend quality time together.

1. Decide what would be quality time for each of you separately.
2. Decide what would be quality time for you as a couple.
3. Each partner lists:

   - Activities that are the most important to you as a couple.

- The amount of time these activities would require.
- Some suggested times to do these activities together.

4. Talk over your suggestions and come to an agreement about which activities you will make quality time to do together on a regular basis.

Loving System #6: Sense of Humor

Sue and Art are trying to improve the quality of their relationship. They monitor any weakness in the relationship. If mistakes occur, they take them personally and then work quickly to eliminate those mistakes. This strategy does not work and they do not know why.

You cannot eliminate mistakes. They are a part of life. Mistakes permit us to learn and grow. The fact that you forgot to do something is unfortunate but not a disaster. If you can see the humor in your own egocentric behavior, it can help you to be less demanding of your partner.

Having a sense of humor means you have the ability to see life in perspective. It is a process of seeing the hidden and positive meanings in each event. One's sense of humor is based on a feeling of worth and self-esteem. With a sense of humor, you are able to debunk any negative nonsense or discouragement.

When a couple has a sense of humor, they can take a disastrous situation, keep it in perspective, and learn from it without blaming each other for causing it. For example, you are at the airport and you ask your partner for the tickets and passports. The reply is "But I thought *you* had them." You can have a fit or accept the situation, reschedule the flight, and go back and get the tickets and passports.

Your partner goes to the store to get groceries and returns after the stores have closed without some essentials. Again, you can blow up or see it in perspective—it's not the worst thing that could happen.

When a person has a sense of humor, it is possible to overcome all self-constricting activity. One no longer needs to put up a pretense of perfectionism; instead, a sense of humor enables one to have the courage to be imperfect. Having a sense of humor as a couple means that the system works in such a way that you will not blow your problems out of proportion but instead look at each challenge with a new perspective. We suggest that every couple practice seeing the humor and the light side of any challenge. This means developing a perceptual alternative to any given situation. If you try, you can see something positive and humorous in just about every situation.

Without a sense of humor people become overconcerned about every little thing that goes wrong. This approach is counterproductive because it places blame on the partner who made the mistake. As we said earlier, mistakes help us learn and grow. Don't get mad at your partner for a behavior that is part of being human.

Look for something positive or humorous in each situation that appears to be negative. Develop a positive perceptual alternative for things you've been concerned about. Use your sense of humor to see them in perspective. Do the following sense of humor activity:

- Identify a situation that appears to be negative.
- Together, look for anything positive or humorous in it. This will give you a perspective on the situation.
- Discuss the value in seeing things in perspective versus tensing up and blowing them out of proportion.

Loving System #7: The Marriage Meeting

Harry and Connie are both executives in their respective companies. On the job they are known for their planning and management skills. Their home life is another story. They leave each other lots of notes; they call and communicate only in emergencies. They never meet to plan anything; they simply tell each other what is planned and when. Consequently, they have no method for dealing with emergencies and the continual demands of a relationship.

If partners are to function in an ongoing relationship, they must spend time together and plan. The marriage meeting is essential for organizing the marital system. We suggest that you and your partner meet regularly at a time during which you will not be interrupted. The meeting can be scheduled on a weekly, biweekly, or monthly basis, but it should be held regularly, according to your needs. Allow thirty to sixty minutes to cover marital relationship discussions. The following three guidelines will enable you to start conducting effective meetings:

1. Prepare an agenda for each meeting. Each partner lists items he or she wants to discuss. The lists are then exchanged before the meeting.
2. Base the meeting on the following:

   • Positive events since the last meeting.
   • A discussion of progress with work and chores at home.
   • Future plans for fun (short- and long-term).
   • Problems and challenges in the marriage or family.
   • Additional items for discussion.

3. Set up the meeting as follows:

   • Participate as equals, speaking honestly and listening carefully.
   • Keep the meeting within the established time limits.
   • Schedule an activity for the future that each partner enjoys.
   • Spend part of the time encouraging each other, pointing out what is positive and what is going well in the relationship.
   • Make decisions jointly. Both partners must agree in order for a decision to be acted upon. If there is no agreement, defer the decision and action until the next meeting.

- Plan a time when you will agree to do things for each other that indicate caring. Exchange lists of things to do that would indicate caring.
- Do not allow the meetings to become gripe or arguing sessions. If there is some griping and ventilating, identify specific issues and develop some positive suggestions. When necessary, use the conflict resolution procedures on page 97.
- Assess progress regarding decisions that were made at earlier meetings.

Marriage Meeting Activity:

1. Take time together to read the guidelines for a marriage meeting.
2. Schedule a time to hold a marriage meeting.
3. Conduct a marriage meeting.
4. Evaluate the strengths and weaknesses in your marriage.

Loving System #8: Marital Self-Evaluation

The items in the self-evaluation that follows are scored from 1 (low) to 10 (high). Identify how you typically feel about each of the statements. Indicate how you think your partner will evaluate him- or herself. After you and your partner have completed the self-evaluation separately, give each other feedback on how your perceptions

match or differ from your partner's (e.g., if you see yourself as an "8" and your partner sees you as a "5," discuss
the discrepancy). Also talk about areas in which your
perceptions are close and empathetic with those of your
partner.

Identify areas in which you both agree there is a need
for improvement. Discuss and identify specific ways you
can improve. Make a commitment to change and evaluate your progress after one week.

Marital Self-Evaluation

Circle the number that reflects how you feel about each
item below at this time:

Positive   *Negative*

10   9   8   7   6   5   4   3   2   1
   1. I understand my   I don't understand my
      goals and my   goals and my partner's
      partner's goals.   goals.

10   9   8   7   6   5   4   3   2   1
   2. I encourage my   I don't encourage my
      partner.   partner.

10   9   8   7   6   5   4   3   2   1
   3. I listen to my   I don't listen to my
      partner.   partner.

10   9   8   7   6   5   4   3   2   1

4. I recognize and understand my partner's feelings.

I don't recognize and understand my partner's feelings.

10   9   8   7   6   5   4   3   2   1

5. I can see the potential in situation.

I am pessimistic.

10   9   8   7   6   5   4   3   2   1

6. My communication with my partner is honest and open

My communication open and honest

10   9   8   7   6   5   4   3   2   1

7. I believe I am responsible for my own positive self-esteem.

I blame my partner and others for my lack of self esteem.

10   9   8   7   6   5   4   3   2   1

8. I plan and communicate my intentions openly.

I fail to plan and communicate my intentions.

10   9   8   7   6   5   4   3   2   1

9. I recognize and choose my behavior and beliefs.

I am a victim of my behavior and beliefs

10   9   8   7   6   5   4   3   2   1

10. I resolve conflict with my partner.

I try to get my way or prove I am right.

10   9   8   7   6   5   4   3   2   1

11. I spend enough quality time with my partner.

I spend little quality time with my partner.

10   9   8   7   6   5   4   3   2   1

12. My partner and I share marriage responsibilities in a fair manner.

My partner and I don't share marriage responsibilities.

10   9   8   7   6   5   4   3   2   1

11. My partner and I have fun in many different ways.

My partner and I don't know how to have fun.

·6·

Time for Intimacy, Sex, and Closeness

Sex in marriage is not something you get or do;
it is how the marriage is and the sheer dreams of
how it will be. It is caring about and attending
to each other more than caring about and
attending to the lawn, the kids, the job, the car,
and the leaky sink. Sex is more a matter of
priorities than genitals.

—Paul Pearsall, *Super Marital Sex*

Intimacy or emotional closeness is the most pleasurable
state that humans are capable of experiencing. Alcohol, drugs, success, or wealth cannot outdistance the joy
that comes from an intimate relationship. Many couples
confuse intimacy with sex and passion. The range of
intimacy varies from couple to couple: Some couples
want to be very close all the time, while others want to
be close only some of the time. With the passage of time,
intimacy increases in a relationship; passion increases initially and tends to taper off with time. Most of us want
intimacy and closeness in a marriage; however, we confuse them with a frequent sex life.

103

Only you can gauge the quality of your sex life. Even sex researchers cannot agree on how frequently sex ought to occur, what percentage of time should be devoted to foreplay, whether sex is best when planned or done spontaneously, or whether or not climaxes are important.

Your spouse does not remain new, young, different, or forever in style, but neither can anyone you choose in his or her place. Many people feel sex is more important than the relationship itself, so when sex works the relationship works, and if sex doesn't work perfectly they feel there's something wrong with the relationship. If we applied this principle to other aspects of our lives, we'd really be in trouble. If we live in the city and yet keep staring out at the beautiful, snow-capped peaks in the distance, does that mean our lives lack something? Of course not. Unfortunately, we may tend to use the times of relating sexually as the hallmark of our worth as an individual and the final indicator of the success of our marriages.

Sex is an important *element* in a relationship. It is not the most important thing or the only important thing. What makes great sex possible is *love* far more than technique, and *mature love is other-centered.* Sex must serve love, not vice versa. Very few people give in a truly sustained other-centered manner, yet such giving is often required to create a meaningful sexual relationship.

Most people will stay with a mate they love even though the sex is not all that great; however, few will stay with a mate they do not love even if the sex is excellent. After all, one may get technical excellence from a one-night stand with no great hassle, but that's all it is—empty calories, a quick fix—nothing more. Real love means loving your partner as is. Love is giving, love is caring, love doesn't keep score and may require the kind of sacrifice where you sometimes give but get nothing in return for a while. Good sex also requires good communication and feedback, because only then can you begin to understand your partner's sexuality and create higher levels of being together.

Many of the problems in a sexual relationship are caused by bad habits. Here are twelve bad sexual habits that you should avoid or overcome.

1. Do you always make love in the same way? Do you do it at approximately the same time in the same place? Would you enjoy your favorite food if all you ate day in and day out was the same food, at the same restaurant, in the same booth?

2. Do you always leave lovemaking until bedtime?

3. Do you fondle each other's genitals too quickly after starting lovemaking, neglecting cuddling together, slow kissing, and caressing other parts of the body?

4. Do you talk during lovemaking? You could be conveying endearments, and even more important, requests, information, and feedback about your wishes and needs.

5. Do you talk about unrelated events during lovemaking? If you do, your partner gets a very clear message that your mind is elsewhere, which is a real slap in the face for someone who is trying to express his or her love for you.

6. Do you habitually not have enough time for proper

lovemaking? Are you always watching the clock and rushing?

7. Do you wear clothing that turns your partner off during lovemaking?

8. Do you make love when you are not clean?

9. Do you always have the lights off when you make love?

10. Do you hop out of bed immediately to wash your genitals after intercourse?

11. Do you only show your partner affection when you want sexual contact?

12. Do you engage in pleasurable physical contact with your partner's sexual organs only when you intend to carry through and have intercourse? Playful genital and breast stimulation should be part and parcel of daily affectionate body contact.

It's easy to slip into these bad habits without realizing what is happening. They are quick ways to dampen sexual enthusiasm and interest. The activities that follow will heighten your sexual interest and satisfaction.

Intimacy Activity #1: Be Informed

Be a true expert on sex. Read books or manuals on the topic. Knowledge is power. However, be discriminating in what you read.

• Buy a book and read it with your partner. Any book is fine as long as it is fiction.

• Each partner should go to a bookstore and select two novels, not how-to books. Also buy different color markers and underline the passage of these books that you find interesting; then exchange books. Make time to talk about the books and the sections that are underlined before lovemaking. Notice your partner's underlined sections when you exchange books. Ask your partner why he or she underlined a given section and how he or she might have felt when reading that particular part.

• Together buy a book on lovemaking. Purchase one that seems right for your life-style after browsing through the range of available books. Alex Comfort's *Joy of Sex,* Maurice Yaffe and Elizabeth Fenwick's *Sexual Happiness,* or Lonnie Barbach's *For Each Other* are excellent. The book you choose should not be purchased solely to provide you with factual information. Its purpose is to help you and your partner learn to communicate easily and comfortably about all aspects of lovemaking and sexual expression. Use the book as follows:

1. Read the first page aloud to your partner. As you do, either of you is free to interrupt, to comment, or to ask a question. At the end of the page, discuss together what has been read. When this has been done, your partner will read the next page to you in the same way. Taking turns in this fashion will allow each partner to be a giver and receiver of information.

2. Put a time limit of fifteen minutes on this exercise, which, if possible, should be repeated each day. A

little each day is far more rewarding than infrequent lengthy sessions.

3. Rent a movie and surprise your partner with it. The movie can be sexually explicit or a G-rated romance, whatever is exciting for you. Take turns selecting the movies.

Intimacy Activity #2: Touching

Intimate focus is used successfully as treatment for sex problems. This program works very well for couples who are highly motivated, who have a reasonable degree of body comfort, and who are willing to spend time with each other.

Intimate focus has four basic aims. First, it helps to reduce performance anxiety, which is the thing that most often inhibits sexual arousal. The more you worry about your sexual performance, the more anxious you feel and the less you respond. In intimate focus there are none of the usual goals or arbitrary standards that can intrude into everyday sex: He doesn't have to get an erection; she doesn't have to lubricate; no one has to have an orgasm. You only have to be willing to share pleasure.

Second, intimate focus systematically challenges the popular myth of the primacy of intercourse. An overemphasis on intercourse is one of the most common causes of sexual dissatisfaction and difficulty. By forbidding intercourse until its third stage, intimate focus helps you get intercourse into perspective as part of sex, but not necessarily the most important or enjoyable part.

Third, by systematically guiding you through exploration of each other's sensuality and sexuality, intimate focus aids the development of a broad and varied sexual relationship. Eventually you will have a range of sexual techniques to draw on so that each sexual occasion includes some sexual stimulation that each of you finds arousing and that both of you find comfortable. This store of information about how to give each other sexual pleasure becomes your insurance against future sexual boredom.

Finally, the nature of the program helps you build up habits of open, direct, and comfortable communication about sex. Good communication is an essential ingredient of a successful, long-term sexual relationship. Communication is not sufficient by itself, as has sometimes been suggested, but it is necessary. Sexual likes and dislikes vary among people and for each person on different occasions. The only way for your partner to know what you want or don't want is for you to tell him or her.

Only you can take responsibility for your own sexual satisfaction. The minimum requirement is that you communicate with your partner so that what happens in sex is comfortable for both of you and includes arousal techniques that work for each of you.

Intimate focus consists of a series of pleasurable sessions during which one partner gives the other tactile pleasure. Pleasuring can include touching, stroking, tickling, massaging, licking, kissing, or whatever is comfortable for both of you.

The partner who is being pleasured must give the other partner feedback on how he or she feels in response to being pleasured. This can be verbal—"I like that," "Up a bit," "Left a bit," "Harder," "Softer," "I don't like that"—or it can be nonverbal. You can put your hand on your partner's hand and show him or her exactly where and how you like to be pleasured.

The partner who is giving pleasure must listen and respond to this feedback. Learn about your partner's sensual and sexual responsiveness. Store away for future use what you learn about what gives your partner pleasure.

You can toss a coin to see who gives and who receives pleasure first. In your next session, change the order. You can change roles within a session, but be careful that you are both having approximately equal time in both roles and you aren't bringing into intimate focus old habits of one partner doing most of the work. To see progress, you should aim at having two or three sessions a week. Less will get you there, but slowly. The length of the session depends on pleasure and comfort. As soon as either one of you gets bored or feels anxious or uncomfortable, say *"I would like to stop now."* You are better off having a good ten minutes than a protracted half hour, although sessions that last in excess of thirty minutes are not uncommon.

The program involves three major stages.

Stage One: In this stage, you pleasure each other anywhere on the body *except* the genitals and, no matter how aroused you may become, don't have intercourse. In this stage you will discover or rediscover how much pleasure you can give to each other without ever having intercourse and without it even being a very sexual exercise.

This stage is important for couples who feel their relationship is lacking in physical expression of affection.

Stage Two: In this stage, do everything you did in stage one and you can now add direct pleasuring of each other's genitals. Still, no matter how aroused you become, you should not have intercourse. Many people really don't know how the other sex likes to be stimulated and often assume their partner will like the same stimulation they do. Everyone is individual, and what he or she likes varies. This stage is your chance to teach each other exactly how you like to be aroused. It is also an opportunity to learn how satisfying sex can be even without having intercourse.

Stage Three: In this final stage of intimate focus you include all of the pleasuring you have discovered in the first two stages and you can now add intercourse. Usually begin intercourse with the woman on top, sitting on her partner, but from there you should explore positions with the usual provision that what you do should be enjoyable and comfortable for both partners.

Note: Each of the later stages includes what was done in the earlier stages. It doesn't replace them so that you again wind up with a sexual relationship that consists only of intercourse.

Have as many sessions as you like at each stage until you meet two goals. First, you both should feel comfortable with everything you want to do at that stage, and second, you both should feel you have learned all there is to know about giving your partner pleasure at that stage. It doesn't matter whether you take two or ten sessions to achieve these goals. Intimate focus is not a race. You are better off taking a bit longer to get through the program and receiving all of the benefits possible rather than hurrying through and missing out on any of the benefits.

Tips for Successful Intimate Focus

If it's your turn to be pleasured, give information to your partner. Use "I" messages, such as "I like that" or "I don't like that." Pleased grunts and groans will also do. Don't expect your partner to read your mind. Talk and share, asking for what you want.

If it's your turn to give pleasure, listen to your partner. Don't use "you" messages such as "You don't like this, do you?" Accept that your partner is the world's only expert on his or her feelings. "You" messages are mind-reading, and research shows that this is often wrong. Use your communication skills.

Don't let old demands, goals, or pressure intrude. The man does not have to get or keep an erection. The woman does not have to lubricate. No one has to have an orgasm. You only have to give and receive pleasure and communicate about that.

Stick to the program. Sometimes people will make what they think is a small change to a program, when, in fact, it has a major effect on the program. Many failures in self-help come from not following the program.

Expect to feel awkward and embarrassed, at least at the beginning, especially if your sexual relationship has become a bit rusty. It does seem silly to have to take a printed guide to bed—"Excuse me, dear, I just have to turn the page"—but recognize that intimate focus is a structured learning program.

Once you have mastered the skills that come from intimate focus, you can use them spontaneously and naturally within your improved sexual relationship. For now, however, you are learning. Don't confuse your sexual enhancement program with your sexual relationship.

If sex is still OK for both of you at present, continue your sexual relationship at other times. If sex has become a negative experience for one of you, it's better to call a halt on sex until intimate focus has proceeded far enough for positive feelings to return.

If you get sexually frustrated because you are aroused during an early session of intimate focus when you should not have intercourse, we suggest you masturbate to orgasm. If you cheat on the program, you only cheat yourself.

Use a lubricant to make pleasuring more comfortable and sensual. We suggest baby oil. It is readily obtained, aesthetically pleasant, and washes out of bed clothes. Warm a little in your hands and then spread it on your partner's body. If you don't like the smell of baby oil, try a scented massage oil, moisturing lotion, or talcum powder.

Taking a bath or shower together beforehand can help you both feel comfortable at being close and can start the mood. Appropriate music and lighting can also set the scene. Using red light or candles will help to make bodies look more sensual and help you feel more comfortable.

Intimacy Activity #3:
Pay Attention to Your Sex Life

Too many couples assume that their sex life will take care of itself. Actually, sex has to be guarded and nourished throughout a couple's life together and, in particular, after the honeymoon stage of the relationship is over. There is nothing wrong with a husband and wife periodically conducting a sexual checkup. Here's seven questions to ask yourself and your partner:

1. Is there anything that could be better?
2. Is there anything wrong?
3. What is good about what we are doing and should we be doing that more often?
4. Am I really enjoying myself?
5. Has the fun gone out of sex and are we enjoying ourselves together in other ways?
6. Do I feel unfulfilled emotionally even though I have had an orgasm?
7. Do we need professional help with a sexual performance problem or to make sex more rewarding?

Periodically, at a nonsexual time, make an overall review of the state of your sexual life.

Intimacy Activity #4: Making Time for Sex

Part of paying attention to your sex life is making sure that you make it a top priority in your life. Don't let sex become something that you squeeze in, after you finish everything else—household chores, duties with the children, work activities, sports, gardening, and so on. At any age, you should regularly set aside prime time, time when you aren't too exhausted, for erotic enjoyment. You should allot sufficient time for it so that lovemaking isn't hurried. Sex is an important part of marriage. It helps to keep a couple in contact and serves as a source of ongoing pleasure and renewal in the relationship. Many couples find it helpful to take turns picking the time for sexual activity. Be inventive and do whatever works to make you both happy.

Part of making time for sex is creating a romantic sexual environment. It is important to have a setting in which there is privacy. For your sex life to flourish, you have to create an atmosphere in which you will not be afraid of being interrupted, one in which you can concentrate on enjoying each other and are able to put everything else out of your mind for the moment. Installing a lock on the bedroom door and teaching the kids that they must knock before entering is one answer. Responsibility for birth control should be clearly determined ahead of time.

Intimacy Activity #5:
Continue to Court Each Other

Most couples stop courting, wooing, and seducing each other shortly after marriage. You can keep the sexual juices flowing in your marriage by letting your partner know that you still think he or she is attractive and special. You can do this by trying to look nice for your mate, by expressing your appreciation of your partner in words every so often, by saying "I love you" unexpectedly, by giving signs of affection such as hugs and kisses apart from sexual situations, by concocting little surprises like a small present or an unexpected set of tickets to a show, or by doing anything that says "I was thinking of you."

Intimacy Activity #6: Fantasies

The majority of experts encourage the use of fantasies in a sex life. Fantasies can be used in many ways. New excitement can be injected into tired sex lives if couples learn to reveal their sexual fantasies and sometimes act them out together. Shared fantasies can also be used as a way to keep sex from getting stale in the first place. You can use fantasies alone or by dreaming up something that turns you on while you are making love to your spouse. Although you may want to, you do not have to tell your mate about your private fantasies. Having fantasies and acting them out may be particularly beneficial to couples who are past the rush of early passions or growing older.

Many people feel that it is wrong to think of someone besides their partner during a sexual fantasy, to think of something they regard as perverted, or to play out kinky scenes from their fantasies. The consensus of opinion among sex authorities, however, is that to do all of these things is normal, common, and often beneficial. The following facts may be helpful as you prepare to create fantasies for your marital relationship.

• Just as it is normal for you to have thoughts about food, eating, and drinking from time to time during the day, so too is it normal to have sexual thoughts during the day. Such thoughts are not meant to be locked up, rarely or never to see the light of day! Never having pleasant thoughts about sex is a most abnormal state. It is something largely of your own doing because you have the potential to control what you think about and a clear choice as to whether you choose to exercise that potential.

• The kinds of sexual thoughts (fantasies) that appeal to or arouse different individuals, both men and women, are extremely variable, in the same way that we all have different tastes in food. Some people are aroused by imagining sexual activities that other equally normal people are put off about, or even find revolting! The same could be said for food. The crucial thing to understand is that whatever sexual thoughts or imaginings appeal to you are normal and fine. Thoughts are only thoughts and can't be abnormal! Only actual *doing* behavior can be abnormal, and there is a world of difference between thinking about or imagining something and actually doing it.

• Imagining something does not put you at dire risk of doing it! Should you be concerned that if you allow your erotic imagination free reign you might be unfaithful, or become promiscuous, or lose control of yourself sexually, stop worrying. You will continue to exercise your normal control over your behavior.

• Many women, perhaps even a majority, *need* to use a deliberate fantasy of some kind during lovemaking with their partner, at least occasionally, if they are to have any chance of becoming aroused enough to reach orgasm. This is normal. Women seem to need deliberate sexual fantasy during lovemaking much more than men, although as men get older, they, too, increasingly *need* deliberate fantasy to override some of the effects of aging.

• Contrary to a popular misconception, an arousing sexual fantasy *does not* have to involve you with a different partner or require you to perform unusual or amazing sexual acts. For example, many people find their most arousing fantasies involve a mental replay of a very enjoyable past lovemaking session with their present partner. Others find most arousing the thought of conventional sexual activity with their present partner, but under different, perhaps more romantic, circumstances such as being alone on an island paradise.

• There is absolutely no reason why you must share your sexual fantasies with your partner, just as there is absolutely no rational reason why you must share any other kinds of thoughts with him or her! Equally, of course, there is no law stating that you must not share your sexual fantasies with your partner. It is simply your choice.

• You can't expect to get the full benefit from the deliberate use of sexual fantasy until you have practiced and developed the skill. After all, first you have to learn to be comfortable with yourself about having sexual thoughts or fantasies. Then you have to learn how to use fantasies constructively to promote sexual interest and arousal. Finally, you have to master the complex skill of fantasizing while you are actually making love (or masturbating) and at the same time focusing on your own physical sensations. It is something like learning to play three musical instruments all at the same time. It might be confusing at first, but with practice it can be learned.

Today, think of the most exciting imaginary sexual situations you can dream up. Let your imagination have a field day, bearing in mind that in fantasy, anything goes. Make notes on the kind of sexual activities and situations you find most arousing. Next, in private, make up a story involving you that has a beginning, a middle, and an end. Make sure it lasts at least three minutes. As you fantasize, try to pretend that it is actually happening to you now. If you have difficulty fantasizing in this way, it may help to start by looking at some erotic pictures or by reading some appropriately arousing material. With practice you will find that you can actually tune in to a private screening of one of your favorite fantasies when you are occupied in some tedious, nondemanding activity such as commuting, ironing, or typing. Make a conscious, deliberate effort to tune in to a pleasing sexual fantasy whenever you get an opportunity.

The next step is to begin using one of your fantasies during lovemaking or masturbation. Remember, it takes considerable practice to be able to concentrate on a fantasy, and to focus on your physical feelings while you are making love. It often helps to pretend that the sensations you are actually experiencing are really being produced by whatever is happening in the fantasy; this is especially important if you find it hard to actually visualize your fantasy in your mind.

Finally, discuss the whole issue of sexual fantasy with your partner. Discover his or her views, misconceptions, and anxieties. Then consider reading this section together. After you have done this, you and your partner may want to swap some of your favorite fantasies. Always remember that what is good and right for one person may or may not be good and right for another. If your partner feels uncomfortable or negative about the whole issue of sexual fantasy, you must naturally respect his or her views; however, do not make the mistake, under any circumstances, of giving up your personal deliberate use of fantasy. There is absolutely no reason why you should do so, even if fantasy doesn't seem right for your partner.

Intimacy Activity #7:
How to Say Yes or No to Sexual Activity

It is helpful to discuss ahead of time the possibility of sexual refusals and how you will handle them. In all marriages situations will arise when one or both partners will not want to have sex. Partners may get angry at each other temporarily, there may be trouble with jobs or children, one partner may be unusually fatigued or may not feel well, or, for one reason or another, may simply not be in the mood. Experts advise couples to be straight with each other, to say "I don't feel like it" and to give a simple, honest explanation why, so that the partner does not feel rejected.

Unfortunately, most people use devious tactics to avoid sex—staying up later than their mate, working on home-repair projects, faking a headache, or even starting an argument. Instead of saying "I'm not in the mood," they make up excuses such as "I'm tired" or "I have a stomachache." Behind lies and evasions is the feeling that somehow it isn't ever right to refuse sex in marriage and that your mate will get angry at you if you do. Honesty and congruent communication are just as important in situations involving sex as in other aspects of the relationship.

Respect each other's right to occasionally not feel like making love and make a pact ahead of time to not be afraid to tell each other the truth. Agree to avoid evasions or excuses that often create hurt feelings or misunderstandings. Discuss with your partner how you will handle sexual refusals.

Intimacy Activity #8: Avoid Falling into Rigid or Boring Routines

It is important for the couple interested in growth to guard against rigid or boring schedules such as the "only-on-Tuesday-and-Friday-night" or "only-at-night-before-going-to-sleep" or "only-doing-it-in-the-same-one-or-two-ways-each-and-every-time" routines. Although some couples thrive on complete predictability, most find fixed schedules and doing the same things over and over again boring, or uninspiring at best, especially as the marriage ages. Variety and spontaneity to spice things up is important to keep sex interesting and frequent. This doesn't mean that you have to hang from chandeliers, but it does mean that you must dare to be a little creative, even if it makes you feel silly or embarrassed initially. Experiment: Try different positions, different times of the day, different lighting, even different places to have sex besides your bedroom every now and then. Take weekend or one-day minivacations. It is well documented that sexual interest and frequency increase for couples during holidays. If you have difficulties thinking of something new to do in bed, buy a book like Alex Comfort's *Joy of Sex,* which has plenty of suggestions.

Dullness in the rest of your relationship is often reflected in the bedroom, so try to inject new life into your marriage on a regular basis. Therapists often recommend that couples create things to look forward to. Plan a party or a trip. Take a series of dance lessons together. Contemplate doing as a couple anything that is exciting and fun.

Today, make a sex "to-do" list. Identify sexual activities that you would like to do but haven't done yet or haven't done recently. Ask your partner to make a similar list and work together at eliminating items from your lists.

Intimacy Activity #9: Giving Positive Feedback

Part of being a good sex partner means letting your mate know when you are enjoying yourself. You can say, for example, "I like that" or "Keep doing that, it really turns me on," or you can express your delight by making pleasurable sounds instead of using words. Partners learn about each other's preferences in this way and have their own security boosted in return. They know they are doing the right thing. Positive feedback also means encouraging your mate and letting him or her know that you feel turned on when he or she looks or acts in a certain way. It means telling your wife that you think she is sexy or letting your husband know he's a good lover. Positive feedback in the rest of the relationship also nurtures good sex. Too many spouses only criticize each other. They forget to let a partner know about the things they approve of or admire. We are talking about genuine, positive reactions to your partner, in or out of bed, not about false compliments or feigned ecstasy, which lead to problems. Give your partner positive feedback that directly relates to either his or her appearance or something that he or she does that turns you on.

Intimacy Activity #10: Feeling Fit and Sexy

Feeling fit and sexy definitely starts with our own experience and not someone else's opinion. We may need feedback from others for reinforcement, but we won't hear it until we begin to feel it ourselves, and feeling it has very little to do with some objective evaluation of how we look. Taking opportunities to notice your own body and finding ways to compliment yourself are the best ways to begin. What do you do that makes you feel that you look good? Make a list of the activities that you do that you feel make you look good.

Most of us only notice our bodies when something is wrong and when we notice it, it is because we aren't feeling very good about ourselves in the first place. This is true whether we feel fat and flabby, thin and stringy, or just plain sick. Medical evidence suggests that when we don't feel good about our bodies, when we feel anxious and tense, we are more prone to illness. On the other hand, after we decide to diet or to eat more or to see a doctor, we begin to pay positive attention to our bodies that in turn promotes a feeling of well-being.

The first step to feeling fit and sexy is to engage in any physical activity that strengthens and flexes muscles. If you're not athletic, try walking purposefully for some period of time every day. If you are more athletically inclined, add running, skiing, playing tennis, biking, swimming, or an exercise routine to your schedule. Exercise increases self-esteem; it's almost as if our bodies were returning a favor. Develop an exercise that you can do on your own each day and one that you can share with your partner. Share this exercise with your partner today.

Intimacy Activity #11: Taking Responsibility for Your Own Pleasure

It isn't up to your partner to make you enjoy sex; it's up to you. This means first of all giving yourself permission to enjoy sex. A large number of men and women have strong consciences that act as censors, telling them not to take pleasure in sex. Think about whether or not this is one of your problems.

Additionally, taking responsibility for your own pleasure means communicating your sexual needs to your partner instead of hoping that he or she will read your mind, stumble onto what you want, or divine your needs miraculously. Taking responsibility also means being active during sex, initiating sex when you feel "horny" instead of always waiting for your partner to start things, changing to positions you enjoy instead of only going along with your mate's activity, and making suggestions instead of having no ideas of your own about lovemaking. It may also mean educating yourself more about sex. There are plenty of good books on the subject to help widen your horizons.

Taking responsibility for your own sex life means breaking sexual deadlocks, too. Initiate changes yourself. If you or your mate is no longer interested in sex, if either of you has a sexual dysfunction that persists, if something in the relationship is poisoning sex, do something about it. Instead of feeling sorry for yourself or resentful toward your mate, instead of heroically enduring a sexual problem or waiting for your partner to say or do something, take matters into your own hands. Contact a qualified sexual therapist or psychotherapist or your medical doctor and see what can be done to make things better. Start talking about the problem. Blaming or remaining silent will not solve the problem.

Husbands and wives who have lost sexual interest generally blame their partner; however, people have much more control over whether they are turned on or not than they realize. People who often indicate that they are turned off are usually turning themselves off without realizing it. Something about the other person evokes this wish not to have sex and they then turn themselves off. It is possible to consciously control this behavior and to change these feelings.

What can you do to turn yourself on sexually more often?

·7·

Maintaining Your Relationship

C ommitment, involvement, and full participation are the key concepts basic in every successful marriage. The commitment that every couple makes on their marriage day is seldom remembered and renewed. Promises made at the beginning of a relationship tend to dissolve and fade over time. The excitement and enthusiasm that stimulated the marriage initially are reduced through the many changes that occur in the relationship.

As a couple matures, involvement shifts from focusing on the relationship to focusing on children, careers, education, social activities, religion, sports, or other interests. Faced with all the alternatives available, the marriage, unfortunately, becomes a low priority.

At one time love was considered to be sufficient to maintain any marriage. Many marriages are able to be maintained through verbal expressions of love or physical intimacy; however, emotional and psychological intimacy, the most difficult of all intimacies to experience, has often not occurred.

Traits that make up emotional and psychological intimacy in satisfying relationships include the following:

• Flexibility: The ability to change and tolerate
change. Partners in flexible marriages take responsibility
for their behavior and do not blame others. They respect
individuality and choices.

• Acceptance: The ability to live with the unchange-
able, to live with conflict that is not resolved. Partners in
satisfying marriages accept and live with the knowledge
that there are basic conflicts involving personality differences or habits that will perhaps never be resolved. Self-
acceptance and acceptance of the marital system create
the courage to be imperfect, to accept a less than perfect
relationship. They find satisfaction in their willingness to
respect each other and to honor rather than fight uniqueness.

• Permanence: The assumption that something will
last forever. Partners in satisfying marriages do not seri-
ously consider divorce to be an option at any time. They
may be distant and angry, upset and not communicating
well at times, but divorce is not an option for them.

• Trust: Outbursts of negative feelings or anger do
not destroy the relationship. The partners believe that
growth occurs from the encounters between spouses.
There is belief and faith that each person is interested in
the good of the partner.

• Shared power: There are slight differences in overt
power. Partners in this type of healthy relationship do
not need to fight for power. At their best, couples can
share and exchange roles, (i.e., speak and listen, teach

and be taught, be aggressive and supportive, volatile and calm).

• Ability to live in the present: The ability to look at situations and individuals and to see new ways of achieving goals that are mutually compatible. Partners are not restricted by events of the past but use them as a guide to find new ways of relating.

• Ability to negotiate: The ability to discuss, negotiate, and resolve differences. Each partner understands the other's feelings; they care. Goals are considered and aligned, and decisions are made preferably by consensus.

• Shared positive feelings: The ability to observe, recognize, and affirm the positive. The partners regularly focus on and emphasize sharing the positive.

Couples today have many problems that are the result of the challenge of learning to live as equals. The type of "equal" relationship that we are talking about here is one in which partners have equal rights to develop as individuals as well as to take care of themselves. Each partner shares responsibility for the success and the survival of the relationship. Decisions about responsibilities are usually made after considering the abilities, likes, and dislikes of each partner. It is important to analyze your marriage to see if you have developed a relationship in which each partner feels he or she is equal to the other.

Guidelines for Equality

Here are some guidelines to consider when evaluating the equality in your relationship. Check yes if the guideline applies to your relationship, no if it does not. Identify yourself first and then your partner.

	Yes	*No*
1. I am independent but also cooperative and interdependent.	___	___
2. I am capable of close intimate relationships without clinging.	___	___
3. I am able to show strength by sharing or assuming responsibility for certain decisions and allowing my partner to do the same. There is no need to dominate or to submit.	___	___
4. I have no great fear of losing my partner.	___	___
5. I do not seek to control my partner, nor does my partner seek to control me.	___	___

Extending Your Relationship Warranty

Currently our ovens and appliances create and produce more warmth for longer periods of time than our marriages. If there is some failure, the appliances are under warranty and can usually be repaired quickly. This is not true of marriage.

We all need to systematically find ways to enhance and extend the positive aspects of our relationships.

The following concepts will create a way for you to extend the warranty on your marriage:

Making your relationship a priority.
Communication.
Regularly planned marriage meetings.
Negotiating change through conflict resolution.
Encouragement and affirmation.
Regularly planned fun.
Sense of humor.

Making Your Relationship a Priority

To make your marriage a priority, you need to take two steps:

Step 1: Take an inventory of all the various responsibilities and commitments in your lives and then place your marriage at the top of that list. Once you do that you will find that parenting, athletics, and other areas will be seen in terms of how they affect your marriage relationship.

Step 2: Check your date book. If you don't have one, get one. In this date book you will list the time for a weekly marriage meeting; times during the week for a regular dialogue with your partner; specific plans for fun activities in the marriage; and times that you will decide to do things that you enjoy together.

Some of you may think that this process makes marriage too organized and systematic. In practice, we have found that the couples that receive the greatest amount of satisfaction and enjoyment from their marital relationship are those that are willing to make a commitment to that relationship, not only verbally but in actual time. Unless you are willing to put marriage maintenance on your schedule, just as you do your child's Little League practice, your daughter's dance or music lesson, or your dental appointment, you will not understand the importance of taking time for love. It was obviously important to make time for love when you first met and were courting. Now it is even more important.

Communication

Communication is the process of regularly and consistently making yourself open, honest, and congruent to your partner. As we have suggested in this book, set aside a minimum of ten minutes a day for dialogue. This would allow a minimum of five minutes for each of you to express your feelings. If you become comfortable with the dialogue you may want to extend the time period.

When one person talks, the other listens and does not comment. You share what you are experiencing at this point in time—your beliefs, feelings, goals, and values. Through this process each of you will gain a deeper understanding of yourself and your partner.

Why do we place such importance on regular and consistent dialogue? Dialogue is as crucial to your relationship as gas is to an automobile or airplane. It's as essential as wind is to a sailboat. In simple terms, little positive movement will occur without dialogue; it is through dialogue that people begin to share what is on their minds and hearts—their anxieties, their joys, their sorrows, their goals, their feelings, both positive and negative. By continual sharing you bring a new enthusiasm, energy, and a vitality into the relationship.

Dialogue is the basis of increasing communication and strength in the relationship. The communicating relationship of a couple needs to be checked regularly. You can do this by asking yourself these simple questions:

- Am I honestly and openly expressing both my thoughts and feelings?
- Am I regularly becoming more congruent?
- Are my attitudes and beliefs promoting open communication, or do I have limiting beliefs such as "I am right," "It's your problem," or "Talk will only make it worse"?
- Do I share my feelings?
- Do I share my intentions?
- Do I affirm myself?
- Do I encourage my partner?
- Are we both open to feedback?

Just as you check whether your car is low on oil, you must check whether your communication is low on energy and enthusiasm. Open communication avoids building up unshared feelings or complaints. The simple guidelines listed here, as well as others discussed in this book, will help you to maintain your marriage.

Regularly Planned Marriage Meetings

We believe in the importance of regularly scheduled marriage meetings. Schedule these meetings at a time when you will not be interrupted. Set forth the minimum amount of time you feel will be productive, anywhere from thirty minutes to one hour.

Each meeting needs an agenda of items to be discussed. This agenda needs to be posted prior to the meeting and should be kept in a notebook. Include the following points:

What I like about our relationship, what I like that I am doing, and what I like that my partner is doing.

What I would like to see improve in the relationship or what I think could go better.

What I am willing to do to improve the relationship.

Positive things I like in the relationship.

A discussion of work and chores.

Plans for fun.

Problems and challenges.

At other times you may want to use the Marriage Assessment on pages 12–15, which consists of fifty items related to thoughts, feelings, behavior, system, and intimacy. This will also help you to identify areas that need work in your relationship.

At the marriage meeting, each partner will speak honestly and openly and listen to the other with empathy. Each person needs to participate as an equal. Plan an enjoyable activity each week that can be shared. The focus should be on encouraging each other by pointing out what is positive and what is going well. Do not focus early meetings on highly controversial subjects that are designed to create conflict in the relationship. A marriage meeting is not a frill or an experiment but something that is very basic to improving your relationship.

Negotiating Change Through Conflict Resolution

When conflict occurs, couples have several choices. They can fight, avoid the conflict, or resolve the conflict. Energy devoted to fighting and establishing who is right and who is the winner is seldom productive. Under these conditions the conflict remains unresolved and only reaches another level. When couples avoid the issue in conflict, it usually comes back at a later time in a much more severe form. The only reasonable alternative is conflict resolution. Change is based on the willingness of the partners to deal with the issue. Because conflicts hold real potential for damaging the relationship, it is important that they be resolved.

Conflicts may revolve around a variety of issues. Some frequent causes of conflict are the sexual relationship, finances, recreation and leisure, parenting and children, in-laws, religion, friends, and alcohol and drugs. There is an endless variety of issues that may be the basis of conflicts. A simple but systematic procedure can be applied to the resolution of any conflict. The steps include showing mutual respect and pinpointing the real issue.

Here are some real issues we have identified:

- You feel your power is being challenged. Your ability to control the situation is threatened.
- You feel a threat to your status and ask, "Why should I give in?" Your superiority is challenged. You say, "If I am not on top and respected as such, I am going to feel inadequate and unable to function."
- You feel hurt and want to retaliate or get even. You may have the attitude, "My partner won the last one and I'm going to get even this time." When the issue is decided as to who controls or resents control or who feels a lack of respect, the couple is then in a position to start to consider ways to reach an agreement.

To explore the real issue you need to consider some of your partner's goals and priorities, which may include the following:

- To gain power. In this situation, one partner makes demands to show "I'm in control," usually making the other partner feel challenged or angry.
- To get even. In this form of revenge, one partner hurts the other by either word or deed, causing hurt feelings and confusion.
- To excuse self by demonstrating inadequacy. One partner blames the other for his or her own shortcomings, which makes the other partner feel frustrated and discouraged, considering giving up.
- To conform. Active conforming is taking a positive role toward a goal; passive conforming is more

focused on pleasing at all costs. Sometimes conforming appears to be like perfectionism; at other times it is like pleasing.

- To control. The controller is an individual who thinks he or she is dealing with life's problems by being logical and rational, controlling emotions and actively leading others.
- To strive for perfection. Individuals who wish to control others or conform to other's demands do this by completing tasks in a very conscientious way.
- To be a victim. The victim may show feelings of low self-esteem, discouragement, and low energy. This person is interested in being able to control life situations related to career or peers by being over-sensitive to other people's feelings.
- To be a martyr. Expectations of self and others are so high, the martyr continues to set off situations at work or with loved ones that are characterized by criticism and feelings of unfairness. Solutions include seeking areas of agreement, and participating mutually in decisions.

Encouragement and Affirmation

One of the challenges in any relationship is the problem each partner has with his or her self-esteem. When one person (or both) in a marriage has low self-esteem, it obviously affects the system and the relationship. Very often people who lack self-esteem tend to believe that it is their partner's responsibility to make them feel good about themselves.

In contrast, we believe that when things are discouraging and not going well, you need to take the time to check whether you are taking good care of yourself. We suggest a simple exercise that focuses on the self-affirmation process.

- Sit in a comfortable position; close your eyes.
- Do some easy, deep breathing for at least thirty seconds. Smile inwardly and give yourself a simple positive suggestion such as "I am positive and I feel relaxed." Inhale easily with a deep breath. While exhaling, let your total body go limp. Experience the heaviness and warmth in your body.

This exercise will put you in a position to be even more affirming. To affirm yourself means to value, accept, and celebrate yourself, just as you are. This is a total, unconditional self-acceptance. When you are self-affirming, you actually demonstrate the courage to be imperfect. You no longer need to be perfect, but accept that you will make mistakes and will not focus on them. Instead, you move courageously ahead. You no longer look for people to tell you that you are great or important. Instead, *you* recognize your own strengths. You have no need to be competitive, to prove that you are either more or less.

The self-affirming person ignores any negative self-depreciating statement such as "I am stupid," or "Nobody likes me."

Being self-affirming is being a friend to yourself. Think of a person you treat as a friend. Is that the way you treat yourself? Practice self-affirming by doing the relaxation exercise we suggested on page 138, in which you close your eyes, quiet your mind, and then begin to make the positive affirmations that you actually believe about yourself.

Encouragement can also be extended to your partner. This helps you to celebrate and recognize the positive in both your partner and the marital system. To keep your marriage properly maintained, we suggest that you focus on the strengths of your partner. After you have recognized them, comment positively on them.

There are a number of simple ways that you can use to be encouraging and supportive, including the following:

Listening.
Responding with empathy.
Being enthusiastic and hopeful.

We also suggest that you do the activities mentioned in this book. The encouragement meetings on pages 62–64 and the encouraging days on pages 58–61 are especially important.

Regularly Planned Fun

During the courtship period, the couple spends a lot of time doing things that are mutually enjoyable. They have lots of time planned together, places to go, and things to do and share.

Once married, however, interference surfaces from jobs, in-laws, and eventually children and other responsibilities. A regular part of the marriage relationship involves planned time for activities that both you and your partner enjoy, as well as planned time for activities that may not interest your partner. At the regular weekly marriage meeting, you should schedule activities you may be doing together or separately during the coming week—for example, attending or rehearsing plays or musicals, or watching or playing sports such as golf, tennis, volleyball, walking, or hiking.

Sense of Humor

Here's an interesting brief story. Two pastors are speaking with each other. One asks, "What has God been doing since he created the world? After all, it took only seven days." The other answers, "He's been working on getting men and women to live together joyfully and lovingly in marriages, and that's a much bigger task."

The "me" generation has fostered an emphasis on narcissism and selfishness. The emphasis has been on putting the individual's needs and wants first at all costs. When a narcissistic person becomes part of the marital system, his or her needs are in direct conflict with the building of a loving relationship.

It's important to have a sense of humor about the marital situation. We don't suggest laughing at or ridiculing your partner. The sense of humor we mean is one that enables you to see yourself in perspective. You see your own mistakes, ways in which you create difficulty for yourself in the relationship. Tension in the relationship develops when you feel you are right or that things must go your way. By recognizing the humor in your ego and inflexibility, you begin to see ways in which you may relate more effectively.

A sense of humor enables spouses to see themselves and their relationships in perspective. They recognize that an ego valued more than the marital system interferes with problem solving in a give-and-take spirit. There should be less emphasis on "I" and "mine," less blowing things out of proportion and demanding, and more willingness to see things in perspective and more cooperation.

A sense of humor enables us to see things with fewer dramatic overtones and to lighten up and reduce the need to "win at all costs." The partner with a sense of humor is able to see all time in perspective. What is in the past has happened and cannot be changed by worry and overconcern. The person with a sense of humor sees the comedy in overdramatizing the past or future and chooses to live in the here and now.

By replacing ego with a willingness to cooperate, you will be free to see marriage for what it is—an opportunity to develop a loving relationship.

The Marital Satisfaction Index (see page 142) is designed to help the couple become aware of areas of satisfaction and dissatisfaction within the marriage. It also provides an opportunity for each spouse to "guess" how satisfied his or her partner feels.

When areas of low satisfaction are identified, it is important to find out if the spouse understands accurately the intensity of the dissatisfaction. If both partners are aware, they can explore what each person can do to help

Marital Satisfaction Index

Rate satisfaction in each area on a scale of 1 to 10.
(1 = poor, 5 = average, 10 = excellent)

	Wife Rating Self	Husband Rating Wife's Satisfaction	Discrepancy in Rating Between Wife & Husband	Husband Rating Self	Wife Rating Husband's Satisfaction	Discrepancy in Rating Between Husband & Wife
Work in home occupation						
Friendship (male or female)						
Social interaction with spouse						
Love, marriage						
Demonstrations of affection						
Spiritual or meaning in life						
Leisure and recreation						
Family finances						
Parenting						

reduce the dissatisfaction in this area, for example, helping with work, providing relief from the task, or being more supportive. The task is to identify ways in which each partner can change his or her thoughts, beliefs, attitudes, feelings, and behaviors.

If the spouse does not understand the intensity of the dissatisfaction, the couple needs to focus on the gaps in the communication system that permit this lack of understanding to occur. Lack of satisfaction frequently has a variety of causes. Each partner has to be responsible for increasing his or her satisfaction when it may involve beliefs and attitudes. Couples can increase satisfaction as they work together on areas in which there is considerable lack of satisfaction.

Marriage Assessment

Now that you have completed the lessons and exercises in this book, retake the Marriage Assessment. Remember, the Marriage Assessment is a structured opportunity to tell the truth to yourself about the kind of marital relationship you have. This is not a test, there are no trick questions, and the answers will have meaning only for you. See how you score this time compared to when you took it at the beginning of the book. When you have completed it you will probably still have some specific areas that need work in your relationship. This is normal. As we have said before, marriage is a continually challenging relationship.

Here's how it works. By the end of this exercise you will have answered fifty questions. To begin, read the following statements and give yourself points for each one accordingly:

5 = This statement is always or almost always true of
      me.
4 = This statement is often true of me.
3 = This statement is sometimes, about half, true of
      me.
2 = This statement is seldom true of me.
1 = This statement is never or almost never true of
      me.

Answer the following questions:

A. Thoughts

_____ 1. I think of my partner with positive thoughts.

_____ 2. I respect my partner's decisions and choices.

_____ 3. I am proud of my partner and can accept him/
         her as he/she is.

_____ 4. I am able to change my negative thoughts into
         positive ones.

_____ 5. I take responsibility for the state of my mar-
         riage.

_____ 6. I believe satisfaction is more important than
         perfection.

_____ 7. I am able to choose my thoughts instead of
         merely reacting.

_____ 8. I am able to identify many ideas, beliefs, feel-
         ings, and goals that are similar to my partner's.

_____ 9. I am able to affirm myself and I do so each day.
         I use positive self-talk.

_____ 10. I am able to identify and talk back to my nega-
          tive thoughts.

_____   Total Part A

B. *Feelings*

____ 1. I am in charge and take responsibility for my feelings.

____ 2. I am empathetic and understand my partner's feelings.

____ 3. I am able to change my feelings to see the positive in a situation.

____ 4. I am able to process anger effectively with my partner.

____ 5. I speak my feelings honestly and say what I feel to my partner.

____ 6. I use "I" messages whenever appropriate, sharing my feelings directly, instead of using "you" messages that blame my spouse.

____ 7. I share my feelings on a regular basis with my partner.

____ 8. I am able to focus on feelings of love.

____ 9. I can express feelings with words, touch, or in writing to my partner.

____ 10. I can create positive feelings whenever I choose.

____ Total Part B

C. *Behavior*

____ 1. I encourage my partner each day.

____ 2. I can identify behaviors in myself and my partner that please me.

____ 3. I hug my partner daily.

____ 4. I practice daily encouragement meetings with my partner.

____ 5. I show my appreciation for my partner daily.

_____ 6. I often leave "I love you" notes and other thoughtful gifts.

_____ 7. I communicate nonverbally in positive ways to my partner.

_____ 8. I take time each day to value myself.

_____ 9. I have fun and enjoyment when I'm with my partner.

_____ 10. I plan a surprise for my partner at least once each month.

_____ Total Part C

D. System

_____ 1. I spend ten minutes each day in dialogue with my partner.

_____ 2. I can resolve conflict with my partner in a manner that is mutually satisfying.

_____ 3. I show respect to my partner.

_____ 4. I pinpoint the real issues in our conflicts.

_____ 5. I work through conflicts with my partner.

_____ 6. I participate mutually in problem solving with my partner.

_____ 7. I spend quality time with my partner.

_____ 8. I hold a weekly marriage meeting with my partner.

_____ 9. I can identify ten ways my partner can show he/she cares for me.

_____ 10. I express laughter and humor daily.

_____ Total Part D

E. Intimacy

_____ 1. I am well informed on sexuality and lovemaking.

_____ 2. I feel comfortable touching and being touched by my partner.

_____ 3. I feel comfortable discussing sex with my partner.

_____ 4. I regularly make time for sex and lovemaking.

_____ 5. I continue to "court" my partner.

_____ 6. I regularly have sexual fantasies and communicate them to my partner.

_____ 7. I feel comfortable saying no occasionally to my partner's request for sex.

_____ 8. I avoid falling into rigid and/or boring sexual routines.

_____ 9. I take responsibility for my own sexual pleasure.

_____ 10. I feel fit and sexy.

_____ Total Part E

When you have finished, add up your point totals for each section. Fifty points are possible in each section. You can see which of the five areas are strong and which need work. After you have identified what area needs work (thoughts, feelings, behavior, systems, intimacy), analyze and identify which items need the most work. Identify which of these items or activities you can most readily improve. Commit yourself to consistent improvement.

Meet with your spouse to share actions you intend to take to enrich your marriage. As you take action, the recipient of the action needs to recognize and encourage the positive movement. Remember to affirm yourself for positive change.

Marriage Assessment is a simple, practical way to keep your relationship working smoothly.

This book has provided you with a wealth of ideas and options to build a marriage that is satisfying and enriching. Every relationship has the potential for:

Intimacy or distance and loneliness.
Joy or despair.
Sharing or silence and withdrawal.
Affirming or attacking.
Being responsible or blaming.
Listening or being insensitive.

We have presented the options. You can acquire the skills with practice. The type of relationship you have is your choice. Choose wisely and lovingly.

Bibliography

Chapter 1
Dinkmeyer, D., and J. Carlson. 1984. *Training in Marriage Enrichment.* Circle Pines, Minn.: American Guidance Service.

Chapter 5
Mace, D. 1982. *Love and Anger in Marriage.* Grand Rapids, Mich.: Zondervan.

Chapter 6
Barbach, L. 1982. *For Each Other: Sharing Sexual Intimacy.* New York: Doubleday.
Comfort, A. 1988. *The Joy of Sex.* New York: Pocket Books.
Pearsall, P. 1987. *Super Marital Sex.* New York: Doubleday.
Prather, H., and G. Prather. 1988. *A Book for Couples.* New York: Doubleday.
Yaffe, M., and E. Fenwick. 1988. *Sexual Happiness: A Practical Approach.* New York: Henry Holt.

Chapter 7
Beavers, W. R. 1988. Attributes of the healthy couple. *Family Therapy Today* 3 (January), no. 1: 1–4.
Klagsbrun, F. 1985. *Married People: Staying Together in the Age of Divorce.* New York: Bantam.

Index

151

Index

About the Authors

DR. DON DINKMEYER is an author, consultant, and licensed psychologist. He has received national recognition for his *Systematic Training for Effective Parenting* series. With his coauthor, Dr. Jon Carlson, he wrote *Time for a Better Marriage* and the *Training in Marriage Enrichment* program. His workshops have taken him to forty-six states and to Europe, Canada, Japan, Australia, and South America. He has received professional honors from the North American Society of Adlerian Psychology and the American Association of Counseling and Development for contributions to psychology and counseling. He is a member of the *USA Today* Parenting Panel.

Dr. Dinkmeyer earned his M.A. from Northwestern University and his Ph.D. from Michigan State University. He is a Diplomate in Counseling Psychology and a Diplomate in Marriage and Family Therapy. Dr. Dinkmeyer is president of the Communication and Motivation Training Institute in Coral Springs, Florida. He is on the faculty of the Alfred Adler Institute in Chicago.

DR. JON CARLSON is a psychologist with the Lake Geneva, Wisconsin, Wellness Clinic. He is on the faculties of the Alfred Adler Institute of Chicago and the Medical College of Wisconsin. Dr. Carlson holds a Diplomate in Marriage and Family Therapy from the American Board of Family Psychology and is a clinical member of the

American Association of Marriage and Family Therapy. He edits the journal *Individual Psychology: The Journal of Adlerian Theory, Research, and Practice* and has authored twelve books and more than fifty professional articles. Dr. Carlson has also coauthored the educational programs *Training in Marriage Enrichment* and *PREP for Effective Family Living*. Dr. Carlson has been married for more than twenty years and is the father of five children.